How to Understand Yourself

HOW TO

UNDERSTAND

YOURSELF

**Psychological tests and questionnaires
to develop emotional intelligence**

Published in 2026 by The School of Life
930 High Road, London, N12 9RT

Authorised representative in the EEA:
The School of Life Amsterdam, Frederiksplein 54,
1017 XN, Amsterdam, Netherlands

Copyright © The School of Life 2026

Designed and typeset by Ryan Bartaby
Printed in Latvia by Livonia Print

A proportion of this book has appeared online at
www.theschooloflife.com/articles

Every effort has been made to contact the
copyright holders of the materials reproduced
in this book. If any have been inadvertently
overlooked, the publisher will be pleased to
make restitution at the earliest opportunity.

The School of Life publishes a range of books
on essential topics in psychological and
emotional life, including relationships, parenting,
friendship, careers and fulfilment. The aim is
always to help us to understand ourselves better
– and thereby to grow calmer, less confused
and more purposeful. Discover our full range
of titles, including books for children, here:
www.theschooloflife.com/books

The School of Life also offers a comprehensive
therapy service, which complements,
and draws upon, our published works:
www.theschooloflife.com/therapy

www.theschooloflife.com

ISBN 978-1-916753-22-8

10 9 8 7 6 5 4 3 2 1

CONTENTS

Introduction

It's one of the paradoxes of the way we are made that we, the ultimate owners of our minds and bodies, cannot easily understand very much of who we are. Secure knowledge of our tastes, feelings, characters, intentions and beliefs can be extremely hard to come by; our dreams continually surprise us; consciousness contains objects we can barely name or knowingly experience. It can be the work of a lifetime to determine certain very basic-sounding things about ourselves (many of which would strike a moderately curious outside observer within a minute or two of coming into our company).

If we let things take their unhampered course, we may – with a lot of time – eventually collide with one or two insights about our true natures. A five-year relationship may, for example – after multiple crises and a very painful breakup – eventually throw up the insight that we are 'avoidantly attached' or 'bad at setting boundaries'. A setback at work that costs us our livelihood and reputation might gingerly teach us that we have difficulties around authority, perhaps because of our relationship with our father in early childhood. We might be nearing our eighth decade before we make the discovery that we have tended to blame people unfairly for failing to show us a vulnerability that – we now see – we have been in flight from ourselves. It is all dispiritingly slow. We go to the grave with most of who we are still sunk in darkness; we die before knowing who we have been.

It is this appalling and costly ignorance that the discipline known as psychology wrestles with. Many psychologists have, over the past century or so, set themselves the task of creating tools that can speed up the acquisition of self-awareness, so as to spare us one or two agonies – and decades. They have created questionnaires, profiles and quizzes that attempt to lead the mind to give up certain of its secrets slightly more swiftly than usual. With the help of an artificial prompt – it might be a picture, a word, a scenario or a set of numbers – a responder is allowed to notice certain hard-to-see traits and inclinations. Psychological tests – some of the best of which have been collected here – are, in essence, trying to forewarn us of our identities, in the hope of ensuring that we will not have to stumble quite so blindly and destructively through our lives.

This book is a compendium of interesting, lively, intriguing and sometimes a little eccentric psychological questionnaires and exercises for the reader to discover and complete. The tests range across topics: some are interested in finding out how 'neurotic' you might be; others indicate your levels of anxiety, depression, anger or self-esteem. There are questionnaires about your attachment style, your capacity to express your emotions and your tendency to blame others.

The outward simplicity of some of these tests has historically often prevented thoughtful people from engaging overly deeply with them. It can feel a little offensive to imagine that we may have ruined a marriage or a career for want of a piece of information that could have been extracted from us by a four-minute exercise written in simple prose. But we shouldn't compound our ignorance with misplaced pride. We may have to accept with grace that some of the information with the power to save us could be identified with the right sort of psychological tool in only a few moments. We are creatures who can be killed by a coin dropped from a four-storey building or a coconut blown by a hardy gust. Our emotional vulnerability is just as acute. We don't, on top of it all, have to compound our errors by making ourselves more mysterious than we already are.

The point of the tests that follow is as simple-sounding as it is momentous and dignified: to spare us time; to introduce us at speed to central aspects of ourselves; to teach us a bit more about who we are before it is too late.

DREAMS AND PROJECTIONS

1. The Word Association Test

One of the most significant discoveries of the early 20th century was of a part of the mind we now call 'the unconscious'. It came to be understood that what we know of ourselves in ordinary consciousness comprises only a fraction of what is actually at play within us. Much of what we really want, feel and are lies in a penumbra that we can only hope to dispel with patient and compassionate exploration.

In *The Interpretation of Dreams*, first published in Vienna in 1900, Sigmund Freud detailed the mind's restless attempts to hide many of its most salient truths from itself in the form of dreams that might shock, disturb or excite us while they unfolded, but which would then be deliberately forgotten or misunderstood upon waking.

At much the same time, across the border in Switzerland, another pioneering figure in early psychoanalysis, Carl Jung, took a complementary but more direct approach. Jung understood that many of his patients were suffering from symptoms created by a conflict between what they knew of themselves deep down and what their conscious minds could bear to take on board about their feelings and desires. Someone might, for example, lose all ability to speak because of one or two things they longed to communicate to a particular person but were afraid to do so. Another might develop a terror of urinating rooted in a childhood humiliation that they lacked the wherewithal to remember and process.

Following Freud, Jung believed that healing and growth required that we learn to untangle our mental knots and more fully appreciate our complicated, sometimes surprising but ultimately real identities.

In 1904, together with his colleague Franz Riklin, Jung developed the word association test. A patient was to sit opposite a doctor, who would read aloud a list of 100 words. Upon hearing each word, the patient was instructed to say the first thing that came into their mind. It was vital for the success of the test that the patient try not to delay speaking and that they report their thoughts honestly, however strange, random or embarrassing they might seem. Jung and his colleague quickly realised that they had hit upon an extremely simple yet highly effective method for revealing the unconscious. Patients who, in ordinary conversation, would carefully disguise themselves, would, in a word association session, quickly let slip critical aspects of their true selves.

Jung grew interested in how long his patients paused after certain word prompts. Despite the request that they answer quickly, in relation to certain words, patients tended to grow tongue-tied, unable to find anything they could say and then protesting that the test was silly or cruel. Jung did not see this as coincidental. It was precisely where there were the longest silences that the deepest conflicts and neuroses lay. A literal tussle could be observed between a deep self that urgently wanted to say something and a conscious overseer that equally urgently wanted to stay very quiet indeed.

In a given test, the doctor might say 'angry' and the patient might respond 'mother'. They would say 'box' and the patient might respond 'heart'. They might say 'lie' and the patient would respond 'brother'. They might say 'money' and the patient, struggling with guilt and shame, might go silent for a very long time before saying they needed to get some air.

Though it was made for a clinician to interpret, we can gain a huge amount from taking the test on our own and analysing our responses and hesitations according to what we know of who we are. We can use Jung's 100 words as a provocative guide to regions of our experience that we have, to date, lacked the courage or focus to explore – but that might hold the key to our future development and flourishing.

And, of course, where we go blank and decide the test is really very silly is where we should pay the greatest attention.

Word association test

	20. to cook	47. bird	74. wild
	21. ink	48. to fall	75. family
	22. angry	49. book	76. to wash
	23. needle	50. unjust	77. cow
	24. to swim	51. frog	78. friend
	25. voyage	52. to part	79. luck
	26. blue	53. hunger	80. lie
	27. lamp	54. white	81. deportment
1. head	28. to sin	55. child	82. narrow
2. green	29. bread	56. to take care	83. brother
3. water	30. rich	57. lead pencil	84. to fear
4. to sing	31. tree	58. sad	85. stork
5. dead	32. to prick	59. plum	86. false
6. long	33. pity	60. to marry	87. anxiety
7. ship	34. yellow	61. house	88. to kiss
8. to pay	35. mountain	62. dear	89. bride
9. window	36. to die	63. glass	90. pure
10. friendly	37. salt	64. to quarrel	91. door
11. to cook	38. new	65. fur	92. to choose
12. to ask	39. custom	66. big	93. hay
13. cold	40. to pray	67. carrot	94. contented
14. stem	41. money	68. to paint	95. ridicule
15. to dance	42. foolish	69. part	96. to sleep
16. village	43. pamphlet	70. old	97. month
17. lake	44. despise	71. flower	98. nice
18. sick	45. finger	72. to beat	99. woman
19. pride	46. expensive	73. box	100. to abuse

2. Waking Dream Analysis

We spend one third of our lives asleep, and of this span, a good deal of it in dreams, which tend to comprise some of the most astonishing, beautiful and terrifying experiences we ever undergo.

Unsurprisingly, humans have always wondered what dreams might *mean*. For the longest time, in many cultures, dreams were taken as omens or prognostications, placed in our minds by supernatural forces and in need of being interpreted by priests and oracles. Contemporary life, governed by science, heads in another direction. Dreams are nothing more – neuroscientists insist – than the meaningless spasms of the mind's circuits after a day's exertions. That one might seek to remember dreams, let alone make 'sense' of them, has been framed as inane mysticism.

Yet there is one modern discipline that refuses to give up on dreams altogether. For psychotherapy, as for ancient priesthoods, dreams are immensely meaningful, but, importantly, their meaning comes from within rather than without. The dream is a message from our deep selves to our conscious minds; it is an attempt to admit – in disguised form – to a little more about who we are: what we actually want, what pains us and how we would like to change.

For Sigmund Freud, a dream represents a compromise between a desire to know our truths and an equally strong desire not to know. Our minds, always squeamish, are ambivalent about self-awareness; much of what we could find out about ourselves would disturb our pleasant fictions and deceits and get in the way of a comfortable night. Dreams, therefore, both tell us important things and then disguise what they have said. The muddled and surreal nature of dreams – what Freud called 'the dream-work' – amounts to a highly creative way of covering up revelations and turning these into symbols and codes that are sufficiently hard to crack so as not to provoke us unbearably. For example, our mother, with whom we might need to have an argument, could in a dream 'become' someone far less contentious who we once knew at work; a conflict with a sibling might take on the form of a struggle between two animals; our ego becomes a house and our desires objects in a basement. And then, in case this confusion and symbolisation do not protect us enough, we forget dreams soon after we wake; our immersion in our challenging reality is skilfully kept brief and vague.

Despite our investment in not understanding what we dream about, psychotherapy insists that we will grow emotionally the more we can bear to pull apart our dreams' meanings and come to terms with our complexities. We will mature and heal as we develop the strength to listen to what our deep minds are telling us.

But how can we learn to make sense of our dreams, given their oddities and tendency to evaporate within minutes of awakening?

A central recommendation is not to assume that dreams have universal meanings. Unlike what dream dictionaries try to tell us, specific elements – like water or trees or snakes – don't have a single symbolic identity. No outsider can ever tell us what our dreams mean. We are the best available experts, so long as we give ourselves the chance, and the way to hone our judgement is to do something both rather basic and profound. We have to cut up our dreams into pieces and, as we explore every segment, interrogate ourselves for the associations that they provoke in us.

Let's assume, for example, that we dreamt about our partner dressing in a medieval gown and travelling to Basel in order to participate in a horse race – but then we got bogged down in a conversation with a small child who was at the same time the president. It would be hopeless for an outsider to try to make sense of this, but if we give ourselves time, we stand to make important interpretative headway. After all, this is our creation.

We should, the moment we awake, reach for pen and paper and split the dream into its different parts – partner, gown, Basel, horse, delay, child, president – and then explore each element with patience and free-floating, uninhibited imagination. What's the first thing that comes into our consciousness? What have these things meant to us? What particular aspects of our lives may, however obliquely, be being evoked? What, here, do we believe in or fear or love or hate or desire? Almost certainly, as we pause in front of each part, we will discover something that could, as we reflect, connect up to a larger theme in our lives. The dream will almost certainly be adding in some way to our daytime story about who we are; perhaps we will learn that we are more upset about something than we thought, or more desirous, or excited. Often, without anything mystical being meant by this, the dream will hint at something we need to go out and do. It is not an omen so much as a call for us to grow in some way – perhaps to become more patient, less risk averse or more generous.

If we are interested in dream analysis but have no dream in mind, psychotherapy even suggests a small, fascinating auxiliary exercise to get us going. We should shut our eyes and, at speed, *invent a dream*; we should ask ourselves what we might dream about if we could dream right now. In no more than thirty seconds, we should sum up the dream: for example, a dream about a boy in a swamp looking for a light and a rope. Or a dream about a princess clinging to the wing of an airplane. And, as before, we should ask: What does this mean for me? What are the elements here and how do they connect with my sense of myself?

Our minds are far more filled with wonder, insight and knowledge than we give them credit for. We can be grateful to psychotherapy for insisting that we don't invariably and ungratefully throw away all our night-time visions. They may at times contain the voice of a deeper, more honest self, speaking to us in cautious disguise about who we really are.

3. The Rorschach Inkblot Test

We are often convinced that the way we feel about – and react to – events is founded on how things really are in the here and now. For example, we may report some of the following:

I feel very scared because something very dangerous is facing me today.

I feel I'm being judged harshly by the person I'm speaking to because they are moralistic and cruel.

I withhold my trust because my partner is deceitful and unreliable.

However, one of the great discoveries of 20th-century psychology has been that, in certain cases, this isn't what is going on at all. Whatever our certainties, we may be misreading reality gravely, and we are doing so because of our unconscious reliance on a notably flawed bit of data: the lessons of our pasts.

Without knowing it, we are 'projecting' from our lives into situations in the present that may not remotely merit our presuppositions. If we removed the projective lens, we might end up seeing reality very differently – and often a great deal more fairly:

We may feel very scared, but perhaps there is nothing around us to be terrified of.

We may feel harshly judged by someone, but perhaps they in fact mean very well.

We may avoid intimacy with a person, but perhaps they deeply merit our trust.

The reason we project is that we are – without knowing it – generalising about human nature on the basis of certain significant events from our essentially unrepresentative childhoods, which we cannot quite remember but which have covertly altered our assumptions about the world and all its inhabitants. We mistake the specific with the general; we read all men through the lens of our father, all women through the lens of our mother:

In early childhood, we experienced the terrifying, volcanic temper of a violent parent. Now we see the threat of violence everywhere.

We were humiliated by our mother for the first decade of life. Now almost everyone seems to be out to denigrate us.

A father whom we loved and trusted left the family and broke off contact suddenly. Now most relationships feel like they're about to end abruptly.

What is hardest is that when we're involved in a projection, we typically believe ourselves to be wholly justified in responding as we do. We cannot catch our projected content because it grows imperceptibly muddled up with the complexities of the real people in front of us.

It's because of this tendency that psychologists have come to rely on projection tests, the earliest and most well known of which was devised in the 1920s by Swiss psychologist Hermann Rorschach.

Rorschach generated a series of ambiguous images by pressing ink between two sheets of paper, and then asked his patients to reflect, without inhibition and at speed, on what they felt these shapes resembled and made them think of.

The images had no predetermined meaning; they weren't about anything in particular, they were just the result of where ink happened to have flowed. But what they could very productively do – precisely because they had no intentions behind them – was prompt people to draw upon their unconscious histories.

To an individual who had inherited from their parents a rather kindly and forgiving conscience, one image might appear as a sweet mask, with eyes, floppy ears, a covering for the mouth and wide flaps extending from the cheeks. Another, more traumatised by a domineering

father, might see it as a powerful figure viewed from below, with splayed feet, thick legs, heavy shoulders and the head bent forward as if poised for attack.

We can look at some examples of inkblot images and ask ourselves the following questions:

_____

What do I 'see' in each image?
_____

What comes to mind as I explore the patterns? What animals, moods, intentions or signs are there?
_____

(After a few moments of reflection) What parts of my biography might be getting (usefully) caught up in my reading of these abstract shapes? In what way might I be talking about 'me' while ostensibly discussing the random patterns of ink on a bit of paper?

Inkblots reminiscent of the Rorschach inkblot test

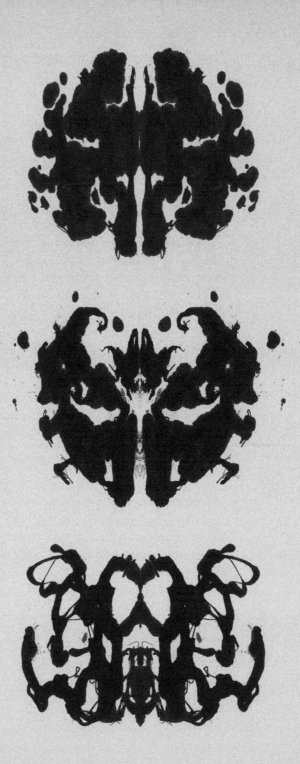

4. The Thematic Apperception Test

In the 1930s, the American psychologists Christiana Morgan and Henry Murray hit upon the idea of using specially commissioned representational images to draw out our unconscious projections.

Morgan and Murray understood that when we look at works of art featuring people whose moods and actions are (deliberately) left indeterminate, we naturally fill in the blanks by making unconscious use of our own experiences. We take our personal obsessions, concerns, lusts, denials, fears and hopes and project them onto the ambiguous figures in the art – and, very usefully, we do this without much clue that this is what we are up to, which prevents us from censoring ourselves or escaping from important but uncomfortable truths. We talk about our real concerns with a rare degree of transparency, precisely because we have no concrete sense that this is what we are doing. We think we're simply telling a psychologist what we believe is happening in a picture; what we are in fact doing is telling them what is going on in our minds.

Morgan and Murray worked closely with a roster of artists to create images that form what is known today as the Thematic Apperception Test. What unites the images is that they all seem to be powerfully about something, and yet their intent is never entirely clear. The images hover fruitfully in a zone somewhere between meaning and obscurity – and on this basis achieve their power to engage our own biographies.

One example shows an older and a younger woman together.

Of this image, we can ask ourselves:

What is going on?

_____

What has happened recently?

_____

What are the characters feeling?

Right:
Card 12F from the
Thematic Apperception Test
by Henry A. Murray

Below:
Edward Hopper,
Chop Suey, 1929

Morgan and Murray noticed (and recorded) how differently people described the contents of this image, depending on what happened to be at play in their unconscious. 'It's perhaps a mother and daughter, mourning together for a shared loss of their alcoholic husband and father,' one respondent might say confidently, making covert use of a sad part of their own life story. Another might assert with equal surety: 'It's a housewife in the process of sacking (more in sorrow than in anger) a very unsatisfactory elderly cleaner.' And a third, wrestling with a legacy of abuse, might explain: 'I feel something horrible is going on just below the surface. The older woman is being inappropriate in her attention ...'

There is never a single truth – only as many meanings as there are viewers. In asking ourselves these questions, we see our own portrait emerging.

The beauty of Morgan and Murray's approach is that it can be put into practice not just on their expressly made images, but on works of art more broadly. Through their example, we are given licence to look again at many classic images and employ them as gateways to psychological self-discovery. We might, for example, consider Edward Hopper's *Chop Suey* and ask: Who are these women? What are they discussing? What has just gone on in their lives? What might the woman facing us want to tell us? After we've answered, we might wonder what part of our stories we just happened to see.

Our society typically gives us a powerful sense that to understand art properly must mean trying to get close to its creator's intentions. But to follow the projective technique is to appreciate another equally legitimate avenue: that the function of art may lie as much in its power to help us explore the shyer or more frightened parts of ourselves.

5.

The Sentence Completion Test

A fundamental paradox of our minds is that they are filled with pieces of information that belong to us but are not known to us – pieces of data that may be utterly critical to our emotional flourishing and capacity for accurate decision-making, but that elude our day-to-day grasp.

It follows that an urgent task of psychology is to devise tools that, rather like the claw crackers and forks served up in lobster restaurants, will grant us better access to the fruitful and salient bits of our minds.

In this regard, we should be especially grateful to a once world-famous but now largely forgotten 19th-century German professor of psychology, Hermann Ebbinghaus. Born into a wealthy merchant's family in Barmen, in what is now northwestern Germany, in 1850, Ebbinghaus was a brilliant student from a young age, and by his early twenties he had set out to explore, through original research, the paradoxes and secrets of mental functioning. He was especially interested in memory, and in 1885 he made his name with a book called *Über das Gedächtnis* (On Memory), in which he named and described what we still refer to today as the 'learning curve' and the 'forgetting curve': models of the way in which information is absorbed, held and dispensed of by the mind over time. Ebbinghaus also discovered what is now known as the Ebbinghaus illusion: a way of demonstrating that we judge the significance of things not in the abstract but in relation to what is most immediately near to them – an idea with wide application in psychology; for example, in the way we judge our status or the severity of a setback.

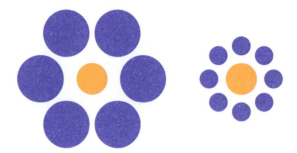

The Ebbinghaus illusion: the dots at the centre are the same size, but the one on the right looks bigger because our minds judge scale by reference to immediate context.

Most importantly for us, it was both in this book and in a follow-up, *Fundamentals of Psychology*, published in 1902, that Ebbinghaus devised a test that was to change how we are able to extract our identities from our personalities. This test, at once very simple and completely revolutionary, is known to us now as the 'sentence completion test'. Ebbinghaus discovered that we could hugely improve our level of self-understanding by completing broad sentences about our feelings or desires, without straining or thinking too much when responding. Examples of such sentences include:

What I really want is …

_____

My biggest regret is …

_____

What I really want to change about myself is …

Day to day, it seems as though shyness or fateful distraction keep us away from grasping these fundamentals about ourselves – perhaps for fear of upsetting the mental status quo, given that our answers are, on occasion, starkly in conflict with the respectable or desirable position on things. Ebbinghaus wisely observed this in relation to two incomplete sentences in particular:

The person I really love is …

_____

If no one ever found out, I would love to …

Here, a married high court judge might answer: 'the coachman' and 'be flogged while wearing my lawyer's gown'. An advocate of left-wing causes might respond: 'the queen' and 'live in luxury'.

The extent to which we hide ourselves from ourselves has since become well known in psychoanalysis, but what makes Ebbinghaus' sentence completion test so compelling is the speed and relative simplicity with which our defence mechanisms can be bypassed and information extracted. A truth that might have required twenty sessions of therapy to emerge in tentative confusion might shoot out of someone with nothing more outwardly complicated or costly than a sentence on a sheet of paper like: *What I'm really sad about is* ...

Ebbinghaus did not properly capitalise on his brilliant invention. This would need to wait half a century until, in 1950, American psychologists Julian Rotter and Janet Rafferty of Ohio State University published what they called the Rotter Incomplete Sentences Blank. Designed for three different audiences – the under-12s, high school students and adults – the test asked recipients to complete forty sentences, including these taken from a test Rotter ran with an adult male:

I like ... to be with people I feel comfortable with.

The happiest time ... I had was in high school.

I regret ... that I have changed.

The best ... thing in the world is love.

People ... are good as a whole.

I can't ... play basketball very well.

I suffer ... from getting too excited all the time.

Rotter and Rafferty's test has become a mainstay of academic psychologists, who have surrounded it with considerable and arguably rather unhelpful complexity. Standard operating rules suggest that one needs a PhD and six months of specialist training to interpret the answers; the manual that accompanies the test runs to 300 dense pages.

But, fortunately for us, the most vital parts of the truth about who we are are readily available to us to see rather clearly the moment we finish any sentence completion test. We don't need a PhD to understand what is going on when we complete:

I would love ...

_____

I am scared ...

Ebbinghaus' invention has spawned what is perhaps the grandest and most condensed of all completion tests:

I am ...

_____

People are ...

Best of all, each of us is our own most accomplished and wisest designer of tests, because we all have a good sense of what we are concealing from ourselves. All we need to do to make major progress in self-understanding is to follow Ebbinghaus and set ourselves some tests under important categories like love, career and family.

Central truths about who we are are waiting to be known, just one unfinished sentence away.

A School of Life sentence completion test

Inspired by Ebbinghaus, we invite you to sit our version of the sentence completion test:

1. Set aside a quiet period. Try to complete the sentences at speed, without thinking too much – that is, by saying the very first thing that comes into your mind, however shocking, direct or emotional it happens to be. Be sure to complete a whole sentence each time, even if the sentence stub is very short. The exercise will pay dividends if you run through the stubs unselfconsciously enough not to let the mind's mechanisms of censorship swing into action. There should be no concern that the answers sound 'respectable'. The stubs will be effective only to the extent that you can surprise yourself into realising what you've 'known but not known' all along.

2. Consider writing down your answers (quickly) in a journal and then return to them for further, slower reflection afterwards. In what way might your answers be slightly different to what you would ordinarily have understood about yourself? What are you learning about who you might really be?

3. For a more light-hearted but also perhaps more confronting experience, consider doing this in company. Set the sentences out on cards in the centre of a table and ask everyone to answer with maximum speed and honesty.

4. Repeat as often as possible; your answers will differ, for the unconscious is never static.

My mother …

I want …

Enough …

I'm so grateful …

The world …

To overcome …

Deep down I …

My father …

If friends …

Money …

In the darkness, I …

Next time, I would …

Sex is …

I don't want …

Happiness means …

Behind the social facade …

I'm furious that …

I'm longing to tell …

In the future …

An achievement …

If I could stop …

If I didn't worry what people …

A good life involves …

If I wasn't so scared …

What people don't understand …

I should pay less attention …

The truth …

I can't ever forget …

My partner …

If I was more …

6.

The Story Completion Test

Extending out from sentence completion tests are story completion tests. In these – which have their origins in the work of the Swiss psychologist Jean Piaget – we're offered the beginning of a story and are then invited to imagine the rest.

Piaget was particularly interested in how children form moral judgments. To explore this, he presented them with a variety of scenarios involving ethical dilemmas. In one such example, a young boy is called to dinner. As he enters the dining room, he doesn't realise that a chair behind the door has a tray of cups resting on it. When the door swings open, it knocks over the tray and all the cups fall and break. Of course, the boy had no way of knowing the cups were there.

Piaget would then ask: Who is to blame? Whose fault is it? Through questions like these, a psychologist might learn a lot about the internal moral universe of the child.

We have reimagined Piaget's approach and broadened it outward. Take the story stubs opposite and try to complete them without thinking too much, in order to release the contents of your deep mind. Make your story very short; we suggest not much more than a minute or so. Relatively quickly, move on to another story.

Observe what themes emerge as you tell story after story. What links are there between the stories you tell and aspects of your own life? Look out for how your stories are both about other people and, in a sense, always about you.

Do this in company to observe and enjoy the contrasts in people's minds. Do this on your own as an aid to reflection and self-analysis.

Once upon a time, there was a fox who …

A teenager woke up one morning to discover they had developed a new power …

With the help of this time machine …

'My biggest mistake,' she thought, 'was to …'

His greatest fear was that …

An old wizard came across a very special book in the library of a monastery …

An exhausted traveller reached an inn at the end of a long, isolated road …

The woman waited tensely outside the office door …

In a peculiar shop with artefacts from around the world, an intriguing box called out to be opened …

Nothing could have prepared him for who he would meet on the train …

He wrote a novel that took the world by storm. It was the story of …

The woman returned home exhausted after …

A boy and his father went out one morning …

Nothing was ever going to be the same again in the family …

A spouse returned from a trip and sensed that something had shifted in the marriage …

The manager left the office knowing …

The old man waited every day for the letter …

He remembered that summer at his grandparents' cabin by the lake when …

She entered the psychotherapist's office with a feeling …

In his notebook, the man started drawing up a plan …

Glancing in the mirror, she no longer recognised the person staring back …

The driver was going ever faster down the country road …

It was the first night after the wedding. In the privacy of each of their minds …

The boss understood that things could not go on as before …

He woke up in the middle of the night after a very strange dream …

She decided to move across the country to …

Sorting through old boxes, she discovered a box of photos …

Sitting across from each other at the table, neither knew how to start …

The scar remained as an ever-present reminder …

As he sat in the attic room, a raft of memories returned …

7. The Similes Test

The simile is one of language's most fundamental and powerful tools: a comparison that helps us to understand one thing by linking it to something else – usually with the words 'like' or 'as'. When we say that someone is feeling uncomfortable or out of place 'like a fish out of water' or as angry 'as a father who can't assert his writ over his teenage child', we are using comparisons to help us define what might elude more straightforward expression.

Psychologist Henry Murray designed a simple-sounding tool to help kick-start conversations with new clients. At its heart is the idea that the way we devise similes doesn't just help us to be more poetic or accurate in our descriptions, it can also be studied for what it tells us about our pasts and our underlying anxieties or hopes.

When Murray gave one patient who had just walked into his consulting room the word 'unhappy', the patient replied, disclosing more in an instant than some might reveal in an hour of more straightforward conversation: 'As unhappy as a poor married man who wants to be an artist but has to wash dishes to support his family.'

Following Murray, we might use the words below as the starting point for our own similes.

	unhappy	
As	disgusting	as
	anxious	
	malicious	
	meek	
	dangerous	
	beautiful	
	naughty	
	deceptive	
	cold	

We might surprise ourselves by saying:

As unhappy as a child who always had to be good to please their parents

As dangerous as someone who keeps falling in love with unavailable people

Like the best psychological techniques, the similes test edges us, with ease and innocence, towards the awkward and important truths we have been avoiding for too long.

8. The Animal Metaphor Test

It can sometimes be hard to think deeply about the conflicts we are facing. Guilt, shame or fear hold us back – which is why Greek psychiatrist Albert J. Levis invented the Animal Metaphor Test.

1. Using a pen and paper, draw two animal figures. Outline the shapes with a pencil or pen, then add colour with coloured pencils, crayons or markers.

2. Write down the following for each animal you drew:

• their age in human years
• their gender
• three of their personality traits

3. Now imagine a conversation between these two animals. What are they saying to each other? Detail their exchange.

When you have completed the test, change gear and ask: What parts of your life might you – in covert form – recognise here?

Levis discovered that people will often quite naturally map their own most conflicted relationships onto the two animals they choose.

A tiger may keep scratching at a rabbit, threatening their life and drawing blood, in the mind of a person enduring a highly imbalanced and tortuous love story. Or a wise, kindly owl might keep being hoodwinked by a rhinoceros, in the unconscious of someone enduring a competitive struggle at work.

Through the help of two animals sufficiently far from us, we may come closer to fathoming what is hurting us most deeply.

9.

The Rosenzweig Picture-Frustration Study

Life is inherently filled with frustrations, but how we interpret these frustrations – what we take them to mean, who we think is responsible for them and how we opt to complain about them (or don't) – is fascinatingly diverse.

One of the best guides to the differences in how we deal with frustrations lies in the work of American psychologist Saul Rosenzweig, who, in 1935, came up with what has become known as the Rosenzweig Picture-Frustration Study. The test consists of a series of cartoon-like images that show people facing a range of vexing situations: someone's clothing has been splashed; a vase has been broken; a fellow spectator's head is in the way at the cinema, etc.

In every case, we are given an empty speech bubble to complete, inviting us to show how we might characteristically behave were the world to trample on one of our hopes.

What the test instantly reveals is that, though frustration may be universal, our responses to it are anything but. When their clothing has been splashed, one person might say with relative nonchalance: 'Don't worry, I'm sure you didn't mean it.' Another might reply in a tight-lipped way: 'It's absolutely fine. No problem at all.' While a third might burst out: 'You bloody idiot, look what you've gone and done! You're trying to destroy me, like everyone always is!'

This test highlights the role that self-esteem typically plays in responses to frustration. The more we dislike ourselves (almost certainly because someone close to us didn't like us very much in childhood), the harder it is to read frustration as anything other than a deliberate attempt to hurt us. Of course people are trying to splash us, given who we are! Naturally, everyone is trying to ruin our experience at the cinema, given that we're not good enough and never were – ever since our father or mother powerfully suggested as much in our preschool years. Wouldn't it be normal that someone would try to break our favourite vase, were they to guess – as they surely can – at the repugnant nature of our soul? Bad things logically and necessarily happen to bad people.

Correspondingly, the more we have been taught – in our first home – that we are fundamentally decent and valuable people, prone to the odd mistake but neither damned nor sinful, the more setbacks can strike us as innocent accidents, rather than plots or retributive acts. Why would someone try to destroy our nice clothes, when we have done nothing especially wrong and have generally noble intentions towards the world? Why would anyone harm a good-enough person? Accidents are far easier to believe in when we don't carry around with us – in pained layers of the unconscious – a lingering sense of our unworthy natures.

Along the way, the test helps us to measure our relative capacities to express pain. Must we always pretend that everything is fine? Or are we sometimes allowed to let out a cry? But what kind of cry can it be? A dignified, bounded complaint that allows us to hold on to our self-esteem? Or a titanic roar that injures us as much as it does our offender, because we have had so little experience of mastering our own anger, and because we have no secure sense of the legitimacy of our dispute? As ever, our past directs our responses: the child who was able to cry for a while, and with sufficient sympathy, when their toy broke or a school friend ate too much of their birthday cake may mature into an adult who can combine honesty with self-control. They neither have to say nothing nor put on a dramatic performance in which all the hatred and injustice that has ever been heaped on them seeks a desperate and sudden way out.

The Rosenzweig Picture-Frustration Study doesn't only tell us how we relate to frustration now. It holds open the possibility that, through self-awareness and much kindly and patient exploration of our childhoods, we may learn to respond a little more wisely and calmly, compassionately and thoughtfully to all the obstacles, large and small, that will inevitably continue to come our way on every remaining day of our lives.

10. The Symbol Elaboration Test

It is humbling and helpful to imagine that we might stumble upon important truths about ourselves by completing a doodle.

Herein lies the wisdom of the 'symbol elaboration test', introduced by American psychologist Johanna Krout in 1950, which is a method for exploring hard-to-reach elements of the psyche through shapes and lines.

Without second-guessing yourself, make your own additions to the five drawings below. Complete or embellish them however you feel is right. You might turn them into animals or machines; there could be breasts or mountains, binoculars or machine guns, hedgehogs or celebrities, warning symbols or charts.

1.

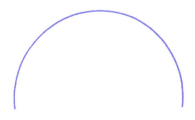

2.

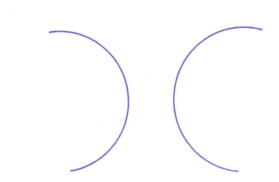

3.

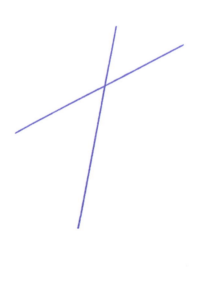

4.

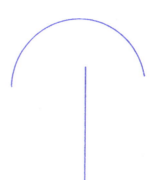

5.

Then, as you contemplate your work, consider the following questions (the beauty of the exercise is that it is a prompt to your own thinking, not a guide to any rigid scientific certainty):

What is happening in the picture?

_____

Who is this about?

_____

Why did your mind go in this direction?

_____

What part of you is present here?

_____

What is sad?

_____

What needs to be heard?

_____

Where do you go next?

We are longing to understand who we are; the impulse towards self-knowledge never ends. We're just waiting for encouragement to take our own modest but crucial messages to ourselves more seriously.

CHILDHOOD
AND FAMILY

11.

The Ideal Parent

We may not think there would be any point in spending time thinking about an 'ideal' parent. After all, we have the ones we have, and dreaming of alternatives, however pleasant they might be, will never change reality.

But this exercise starts from a different place. It asks us to consider how an ideal parent might behave in relation to certain fictional situations. We're prompted to draw not so much on what we have experienced as on what we would like to have experienced if there had been no obstacles whatsoever to our wishes; we're being asked to think about what we are semiconsciously yearning for, as a way to help us understand where we have come from and who we are.

Consider the following:

You've just arrived in the world and are in your first outfit (that was bought just after the second trimester). Your mother is holding you. What is she thinking? What does she envisage of the future?

_____

You're two weeks old. It's late at night. You've just had a feed. Now your father is looking at you sleeping. What sort of man is he? What is he thinking as he looks at you? What future does he have in mind for you?

_____

You're 3. You were trying to reach for a cup of milk but knocked it over. It's gone everywhere: on the floor, onto a book you were looking at and onto your T-shirt. You start to scream very loudly. What does your mother do?

_____

You're 5. You really want to go on another ride at the funfair, but your father says it's time to go. You call him mean and run away from him into the crowd. What does he say when he catches up with you?

You're 9 and a half. It's a quiet Sunday evening, just you and your mother in the living room. What do you and your mother talk about? What's the atmosphere? What do you think about her?

_____

You're 14 and have failed an important test at school. What happens at home?

_____

You're 16. There's someone you really like at school, but they seem not to be interested in you. You raise the problem with your parents. What do they say?

_____

It's time to choose a career. What does your father do and say?

_____

You've recently graduated from university. You feel a bit lost and return home for the weekend. What's the atmosphere like?

_____

In middle age, you decide to retrain for a new career that involves certain risks. What do your parents say?

_____

You have a family of your own. What kind of grandparents are your parents?

Once we've given these questions a good amount of thought, we should then return to each situation and, more consciously than we would have done the first time, wonder: *How would my actual parents have behaved?*

What this exercise understands about us is our loyalty. Few of us like to actively criticise the upbringing we have had. A fierce bond ties us to those who put us on the earth. If we were asked: 'What did your parents do wrong?' or – more acutely – 'What do you resent your parents for?' we would most likely hesitate to answer or even think too deeply. But this is precisely what, in effect, this questionnaire prompts us to do.

The point is not to mire us in resentment, but rather to unblock certain channels of feeling and insight in the name of releasing self-awareness and greater inner freedom.

12.

The Fourteen Vitamins of Love

John Bowlby, the co-developer of attachment theory, proposed a bold thesis: 'It is as if parental love were as necessary for the proper development of personality as vitamin D is for the proper development of bones.' In other words, parental love more or less ensures our sanity – and when it is missing, this can doom us to lopsided development.

We know quite a bit about the vitamins required for our bodies; we're well versed in identifying what might be a shortfall of vitamins C or E. But what precisely are the vitamins of love required by our minds in childhood? We have identified fourteen.

We should get these clear in our minds and then score which ones we had – and which we were deprived of. Consider the following list:

1. A parent has to exhibit – and indeed experience – extraordinary joy that the child actually exists. The child has to feel wanted on the planet. Everyone close by should be happy, very happy, that it has come into being.

---

2. The child has to be allowed to feel and express a range of feelings – not only those that might be convenient for those around the child. It might need to express its weakness and vulnerability. It has to be OK that, for a long while, it:

- isn't impressive to others
- isn't competent in an adult sense
- cries a lot
- has 'babyish' needs

  In order to tolerate this, the adults around the child need to have made their peace with their own vulnerabilities and should not punish in the child weaknesses that they cannot tolerate in themselves.

3.   The child needs to be able to be a child, because the adult is mature enough to have dealt with their own child-like sides. The child doesn't need to parent the adult. A child doesn't have to be responsible or kind beyond its years. It doesn't need to 'grow up fast'. It needs to grow at its own pace. It doesn't have to be any more sensible than it is naturally inclined to be.

4.   The child can exhibit its true self: it doesn't need to develop a false self based on complying to the demands of adults. In its early years, it can give full vent to emotions like fury, envy and fear.

5.   The child doesn't need to people please – in other words, massively adapt to the demands of adults preoccupied with their own agendas. It can become an authentic correspondent of its own feelings.

6.   A child must be given a chance to communicate properly, offering its true views and emotions about things. If it is angry, it can say so. If it is disappointed, it can say so. Its personality is not censored. It learns not only how to speak, but also how to speak up.

7.   Parental figures strive to look at the world through the child's eyes. Physically, but also emotionally, they can get down to the child's level. An adult is very big compared to a child. They need to understand that things that make a lot of sense through an adult's eyes can be very different through a child's eyes. Someone needs to have empathised so that, in time, the child can empathise in turn.

8.   There should be a steadiness about the love that's given. There should be no overly sudden breaks or departures. People should show up on time, day after day, night after night. People should avoid moving to other cities, splitting up or fighting brutally.

9.   A good parent listens properly to a child. A lot of parents think they listen, but it's very hard to listen properly, because a lot of what children come up with is strange and alarming.

The child comes back from school and says, 'I want to burn the school down and gouge out the eyes of the headmaster,' and as a parent, one panics and immediately talks over the child: 'You don't, darling, it's fine. Why don't you go and have your tea?' Now, a parent who's really able to bear the complexity will be able to think: *My child doesn't want to do this, but they're trying to tell me something. They're probably having a very bad day. Can I bear to listen?* Imagine a child in a fancy hotel at the seaside screaming: 'I'm really unhappy here! I hate it here! I want to go home!' And the parent saying, 'No, you're not unhappy. You're actually very happy here. This hotel costs a lot of money.' It's understandable, but this parent is not listening; this parent can't bear the child's reality; this child is not being seen or heard. And so it is likely to scream ever more loudly (the children who scream aren't those who get too much attention; they are those parched with neglect).

10. Parents need to have an internal locus of evaluation. A parent may be waiting for the outside world to approve of the child before they can do so. In other words, they're waiting for the school to tell them the child is clever before they'll think it's clever. They're waiting for the neighbours to think the child is interesting before they can think it's interesting. In other words, the parent can't think for themselves, because no one modelled free thought for them, and so they're unable to model this for the child. Thus, the child grows up timid, cowed and slavish, with a sense that their value is always in hock to the judgements of others.

11. A good parent knows how to be a bit boring. A child wants the parent to be stable. A child needs to feel that the parent's ego needs are being taken care of somewhere else. The parent should not be using their child as an audience for their disavowed narcissistic or exhibitionistic traits.

12. A parent needs to avoid trying to be perfect. If a child feels the only way to be a good adult is to be a perfect adult, this sets up complexities. If you try very, very hard to be a good parent, you may be storing up trouble for your child, who will

think the only way to be in the world is to be flawless. No parent is actually flawless, but some parents try to suggest they might be. And that's very uncomfortable and faulty for anyone to be on the receiving end of.

---

13. A good parent is able to lay down boundaries. It was fun to jump on the bed. It was fun to throw around the cushions. Now we're going to bed. There has to be a no – a hard no. Some lines have to be drawn. A parent needs to allow themselves to be hated. A good parent needs to withstand the child saying: 'I'll never forgive you. I need to eat all the sweets.' Or: 'You're the worst person in the world.' And the parent needs to be able to reply: 'Fine, that's fine. I don't mind being the worst person in the world. I think you need to go to bed now.'

---

14. A good parent has to bear to be forgotten or at least heavily sidelined; that is success. The task is to be superseded. As the child grows up, it doesn't need to feel that it is killing the parent by developing its own life. It doesn't need to feel that its own victories in the adult world come at the cost of the parent's well-being. The parent has to have a sanguine approach to the disappearance of their own job and purpose.

With these vitamins in mind, consider your own experience. Which did you receive? Which ones might you be lacking? At least half the battle is knowing what might be missing.

13. Defences Against Pain

We humans are extraordinarily and painfully vulnerable creatures. Especially in our early years, we are in huge danger of being psychologically damaged by those around us. Damage is, in one way or another, always caused by a shortfall of tenderness and care. As we might put it, it's caused by a shortfall of *love*.

Examples of shortfalls of love are very varied: perhaps at an early point someone went missing or died, someone was cruel or someone misunderstood. It may not have been intentional. It hurt anyway. And, as a result of this deficit, some kind of wound was sustained.

We are also psychologically very ingenious creatures. In the face of any wound, we develop an array of very clever *defence mechanisms*. The purpose of defence mechanisms is to protect us against further damage, to help us to get through to the next stage of existence and to keep us going; *in extremis*, to save our lives. For example:

To protect us against this wound	We develop this defence mechanism
A parent who goes missing	An inability to feel sad whenever anyone is absent
An alcoholic caregiver	Huge independence and self-containment
A depressive caregiver	A resolutely upbeat, sunny temperament that refuses to register downsides
An intensely jealous caregiver	Early retirement from any possibility of success, so as never to generate envy in others

The problem with our defence mechanisms is that they always exact a price. While they protected us very well at a certain age, the more time passes, the more unsuited they become to the conditions we face here and now. What were once ingenious adaptations to a hostile environment become – over the years – the causes of behaviours that limit our chances and ruin things for us.

For example, to add a new column to the table on the previous page:

To protect us against this wound	We develop this defence mechanism	The price of our defence mechanism
A parent who goes missing	An inability to feel sad whenever anyone is absent	Our relationships are shallow and brittle
An alcoholic caregiver	Huge independence and self-containment	We can't depend on anyone; we are lonely
A depressive caregiver	A resolutely upbeat, sunny temperament that refuses to register downsides	We develop an inauthentic, plastic manner; we are fake
An intensely jealous caregiver	Early retirement from any possibility of success, so as never to generate envy in others	We underperform and make less of ourselves than we could; we flatline unnecessarily

It's in the nature of how our minds work that we generally can't see the connection between how our defence mechanisms operate in the here and now, and the wounds we sustained in the past. These defence mechanisms give us what we call *symptoms*.

We have a tendency just to accept these symptoms, even if they're very painful. Often we don't even notice them.

We accept that we're not so good at love.

We accept that we're quite lonely.

We don't notice that we're manically cheerful.

We don't notice how much we're underperforming.

In order to heal ourselves from our symptoms (and the emotional wounds that lie beneath them), we have to learn to understand ourselves better. Our happiness relies on becoming more self-aware. The more we can work at understanding ourselves, the healthier, freer and more creative we can be.

How, then, can we unpick the legacy of emotional wounds? Self-understanding is a seven-stage process.

1. Identify our symptoms

In order to learn how to identify our symptoms, we need to grow more ambitious about who we want to become in the future; we need to scan the present and wonder how things could be improved. We should ask:

What would I like to get rid of in myself?

What fruitless habits, compulsions or areas of stuckness would I like to overcome?

What is more painful than it needs to be?

What patterns of difficulty can I notice, once I look carefully?

2. Identify our defence mechanisms

Our defence mechanisms can be very hard to spot, but it helps to consider a list of some very common defence mechanisms to see if they ring any bells. We might never have thought of these things as defence mechanisms, but we may nevertheless feel a moment of recognition when we hear of the following:

Common defence mechanisms	Underperforming at work	Feeling numb
Falling in love with unavailable people	Being very independent	Hypervigilance; continuous anxiety
Ensuring our relationships always fail	Addiction to alcohol, porn, exercise, work ...	Constant sadness; depression

3. **Understand how our defence mechanisms helped us**

We are used to thinking of defence mechanisms in rather negative terms. They are typically framed in problematic ways, like illnesses that have no rationale. They do cause us difficulties, but to think of them negatively doesn't allow us to understand that they actually have a logic, and its only on the basis of understanding their logic that we can overcome them. So long as we continue to see them as meaningless, freakish aberrations, we will never rid ourselves of them.

We must therefore learn to look at defence mechanisms as highly ingenious, very clever strategies that once would have done a very good job at keeping us safe. We need to look for the *upside* of whatever defence mechanism we recognise in ourselves. We should ask: What was this defence mechanism clever at doing for us? How did it help us? How was it – in its way – very wise and admirable?

Common defence mechanisms	The clever upside
Falling in love with unavailable people	We don't have to be let down
Ensuring our relationships always fail	We don't need to experience loss
Underperforming at work	We don't have to risk generating envy
Being very independent	No one can disappoint us
Addiction to alcohol, porn, exercise, work ...	We don't need to register pain

Feeling numb	We don't have to be sad
Hypervigilance; continuous anxiety	We will spot any danger that comes our way
Constant sadness; depression	We don't have to be hopeful and then disappointed

4. Understand why we needed our defence mechanisms

Next, we need to reconstruct why a defence mechanism was necessary in our life. What was it about our past that would have made it necessary to have our specific defensive strategy in place? What wounds did we sustain? What happened in the past to make life difficult?

We might not be used to thinking in this way. The past may be a long way back now. But we need to proceed like archaeologists who are trying to reconstruct, from the fragments in the here and now, some of the circumstances of a bygone era. Let's add another column and try to fill it in as best we can.

Common defence mechanisms	The clever upside	What wound might we have suffered to make a defence mechanism necessary?
Falling in love with unavailable people	We don't have to be let down	Mum was never there
Ensuring our relationships always fail	We don't need to experience loss	Dad was erratic
Underperforming at work	We don't have to risk generating envy	An older sibling was bullying and jealous
Being very independent	No one can disappoint us	Our parents divorced
Addiction to alcohol, porn, exercise, work …	We don't need to register pain	We were abused

Feeling numb	We don't have to be sad	We were humiliated
Hypervigilance; continuous anxiety	We will spot any danger that comes our way	A parent drank heavily and smashed things up
Constant sadness; depression	We don't have to be hopeful and then disappointed	A parent fell ill and died

5. **Congratulate ourselves**

Now we should do something very unfamiliar: congratulate ourselves on having been rather clever with our defence mechanisms. Far from being some silly, neurotic feature of our lives, defence mechanisms have been an ingenious way of keeping us from devastation. Let's take a moment to feel proud of our smart minds for devising a means of carrying us past danger into the next stage of life. Let's feel compassion and admiration for our defensive strategies.

6. **Identify why we no longer need our defence mechanisms**

Having given ourselves all due congratulations, we now need to do something else: realise that our defence mechanisms are, in fact, past their sell-by date. They were once undoubtedly pretty clever and we can feel grateful to them, but they no longer serve any purpose; now they make life worse than it needs to be. In the circumstances of the present, they aren't required. We can afford to say goodbye to them. Indeed, we must do so.

Let's add another column to make it clear to ourselves how we are losing out because of our defence mechanisms:

Common defence mechanisms	The clever upside	What wound might we have suffered to make a defence mechanism necessary?	What price are we paying now for our defence mechanism?
Falling in love with unavailable people	We don't have to be let down	Mum was never there	We can't enjoy intimacy
Ensuring our relationships always fail	We don't need to experience loss	Dad was erratic	We haven't been able to have the family we want
Underperforming at work	We don't have to risk generating envy	An older sibling was bullying and jealous	We are underselling ourselves
Being very independent	No one can disappoint us	Our parents divorced	We feel so isolated
Addiction to alcohol, porn, exercise, work ...	We don't need to register pain	We were abused	Our health is suffering badly
Feeling numb	We don't have to be sad	We were humiliated	Life doesn't feel very real
Hypervigilance; continuous anxiety	We will spot any danger that comes our way	A parent drank heavily and smashed things up	We are worried sick
Constant sadness; depression	We don't have to be hopeful and then disappointed	A parent fell ill and died	Our spirits are so low

7. | Let go of our defence mechanisms

Now that we have a defence mechanism in view, its logic and its punishing price, we are in an excellent position to carry out the next step: deciding to say goodbye to it. Very gently, we can let our minds know that we can let go of the mechanism that once kept us safe. We can be safe in other ways; indeed, our future flourishing depends on us surrendering our hold on our former defence mechanism.

Once it made sense to be numb; now it no longer does.

Once it made sense to be totally independent; now it no longer does.

Once we had to be sad and fearful; now we can be hopeful and free ...

Now think about your own journey using the headings on the following page as a guide.

A.   My wounds

....

....

....

....

....

....

....

....

B.   My defences against pain

....

....

....

....

....

....

....

....

C.   The price I pay now

....

....

....

....

....

....

....

....

D.   A better way forward

....

....

....

....

....

....

....

....

14. A Timeline of Pain

We try – for obvious reasons – to keep a cheerful narrative of our lives in view: one in which the achievements stand out and our growing confidence and competence take centre stage. But there's a kind of psychological distress that can flow acutely from this otherwise helpful kind of resilience: a tendency not to let our sadness have its legitimate place, and not to appreciate with sufficient compassion just how much we have had to cope with. We are unnecessarily cold towards ourselves because we do not have the full picture of our sorrows in mind.

With this problem in view, we suggest drawing up a personal timeline of pain. On a large sheet of paper, cut up your life into five-year periods:

0–5 years
_____

6–10 years
_____

11–15 years
_____

16–20 years
_____

21–25 years and so on …

Under each slice of time, try to recollect the contents that fit under the title 'What was difficult here'. For the early days, we'll have to do quite a lot of circumstantial thinking. We'll need to lean on what our parents might have said – or not said but implied. The later period will be richer in details.

An answer might look like this:

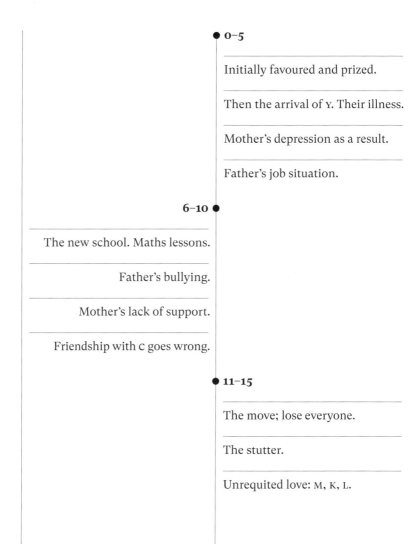

0–5

Initially favoured and prized.

Then the arrival of Y. Their illness.

Mother's depression as a result.

Father's job situation.

6–10

The new school. Maths lessons.

Father's bullying.

Mother's lack of support.

Friendship with C goes wrong.

11–15

The move; lose everyone.

The stutter.

Unrequited love: M, K, L.

After a while, we can see starkly – on a single sheet – something we don't often allow ourselves to think about: just how much we have had to cope with. How hard it has been. How little support we have had. How much we have been holding in. How cheerful we have had to seem.

This exercise opens up avenues of compassion for the self and others. We all have a timeline of pain. Even outside of wars and obvious catastrophes, there is an awful lot on everyone's record.

One of the greatest questions we can ask – something we might structure social rituals around and enliven early dates with – is simply: What is in your timeline of pain?

15. Emotional Family Trees

One of the characteristic possessions of all European nobles for many centuries was an elaborate depiction of their family tree, showing their lineage down the generations. The idea was that the person sitting at the bottom of the tree would see themselves as the product of – and heir to – all who had come before them. The tree gave a quick visual guide to who they were and what others should know about them. If two aristocrats were contemplating marriage, the first thing they would do would be to carefully examine each other's trees.

It can seem like a quaint preoccupation, wholly tied to another age and solely of interest to members of a few grand and ancient families. But the idea of such a tree sits upon a universal and still highly relevant concern: irrespective of the financial and status details of our families, each of us is the recipient of an emotional inheritance from our parents and their parents and their parents before them, largely unknown to us, yet enormously influential in determining our day-to-day behaviour.

We may have done some work in determining what we are grappling with emotionally. What toll did our parents impose on us? What aspects of their parenting are we dealing with? What defence mechanisms and neurotic ways of being did they bequeath us? But we gain from opening the oculus more widely and considering the wider picture: What about our parents? What were they dealing with? What were the forces bearing down on them? What did their parents do to them, and what did their parents' parents do to them in turn? It's for this that it can be helpful to draw a wider emotional family tree.

On a large sheet of paper, place yourself at the bottom in the centre – and any siblings alongside you. Then, on either side above, place each parent, and above each of them, their parents (your grandparents), and above each of them, their parents (your great-grandparents). Connect everyone with simple lines. Your diagram could be holding in mind about a century of emotional experiences, patterns and inherited traits.

Then, get a set of different-coloured pens and fill in the following next to each name:

In red: What they received – the emotional inheritance/ challenges from their parents.

In blue: How they coped – the traits and behaviours they developed in response.

In green: What they passed on – how these coping mechanisms affected the next generation.

We often observe over-reactions down the generations. In other words, the parent who is overly controlling gives rise to a child who is overly free. A parent who is chaotic gives rise to a child overly fixated on regularity and order. A parent who is very loving dies when the child is young, and the child becomes extremely independent and invulnerable. Here are some more examples:

Parent was emotionally unavailable.	→ Child ignores their own needs and becomes a 'therapist' to everyone.
Parent was poverty-stricken and anxious about money.	→ Child becomes a workaholic and obsesses over financial security.
Parent was overly self-sacrificing.	→ Child becomes selfish and self-seeking.
Parent was volatile and unpredictable.	→ Child becomes conflict-avoidant and meek.
Parent was overly protective.	→ Child becomes an extreme risk-taker.
Parent was achievement-focused.	→ Child becomes entirely neglectful of legitimate status needs.
Parent was socially isolated.	→ Child becomes extremely social and cannot be alone.

As we complete the map, we can look for:

Emotional 'allergies' – what each generation was trying to avoid repeating

_____

Pendulum swings – where the correction went too far in the opposite direction

_____

Unintended consequences – how solving one problem created another

_____

Patterns that repeat despite attempts to be different

16. Conditions of Worth

The moment babies are born, their minds are dominated by an urgent question: What do I need to do in order to be loved?

Babies are entirely at the mercy of the prevailing environment, and therefore, knowing what exactly the people in this environment want from them in exchange for keeping them alive is central to their very survival. Furthermore, how this question is answered will shape their entire personality and sense of adult priorities. Who we are is predominantly the result of what we needed to do to capture and sustain the interest of the people who put us on the earth.

There are broadly three answers to the baby's question:

1. Nothing very much

A certain sort of parent immediately makes it clear: the baby doesn't need to do anything to deserve to exist. The baby's own needs come first; who they are and what they want is the priority in those early, fragile months and years.

From such a base, a child can grow up liking themselves, being in touch with their needs and adjusting to the needs of others without too great a loss of creativity or individuality. They don't have to do anything extraordinary to feel they are fine – and if they happen to do it anyway, it will simply be out of a sense of inherent curiosity and appetite.

This is, needless to say, the love we should all want – and should all have had.

2. To earn love, you must succeed

For a certain kind of parent, the baby's existence is premised on an enormous requirement: the child has to help the parent feel better about themselves; they have to help the parent paper over their own inadequacies, compromises and insecurities.

For example, to ward off any risk that the parent might be thought of as stupid, the child has to demonstrate extreme intelligence. To compensate for the parent's lack of a stellar career, the child has to shine globally. To appease the parent's fear of ugliness, the child has to be blatantly pretty. To ward off fears of dullness and the pull of depression, the child needs to be a cheerful comic. The child is a compensatory object at the behest of the parent's disguised vulnerabilities. They are not allowed to be shy, hesitant, confused, quiet or unimpressive to strangers – for all this would devastate and madden an already precariously balanced parent.

With such an upbringing, the child will constantly be left wondering what they can do next to generate applause and acclaim. They will exhaust themselves in the pursuit of a love that should have been theirs from the first.

3. To earn love, you must fail

Some children have to succeed in order to be loved; some – even more darkly – know they must fail. There are parents who will only tolerate children who don't threaten their place in the world. They are not allowed to be any happier, more beautiful or more successful than them – and if they come anywhere close to being so, a vengeful aggression will make itself felt.

The child understands well enough the rule they have been placed under. They can be expected to grow up with tendencies towards self-sabotage and under-performance. If they promise to be beautiful, they'll be sure not to take any pleasure in their physical appearance; if they are on track to do well at school, they'll ensure they always manage to fail the final exam. If they end up with a good career, they'll do their utmost to show their rivalrous parent that it isn't any fun really – perhaps by developing a psychological disorder that guarantees a demonstrable misery.

Sometimes – even more perplexingly – more than one message emanates from a single parent. The parent swings between wanting a child to shore them up and fearing that the child is threatening them. The child will be under pressure to both succeed and fail. There will be nowhere for the benighted soul to turn.

After reading these three descriptions, consider which of them best describes the early parenting style(s) you experienced. Use the following sentence stems to guide your reflections.

How I sought love as a child:

I felt that in order to be loved, I needed to …

I therefore sought love, attention or approval by …

The moments I felt most loved were when …

My self-worth was closely tied to …

I was not allowed to …

The ways I tried to appease the adults around me were …

One clear message I received about my worth was …

Now, turning to the following questions, we may start to notice some patterns surfacing.

How I seek love today:

As an adult, in order to be loved, I feel I need to …

The ways in which I still seek love, attention or approval are …

The moments I feel most loved are when …

My self-worth is closely tied to …

The ways I try to appease people around me are …

One thing I tend to hide in my relationships is … because …

Looking back at your answers as a whole, what patterns can you notice? How are you still – so many years later – fighting to survive?

17. Parenting Styles

The bedrock of a sane and balanced adulthood is laid in childhood via loving and responsible parenting. Our parents may have vehemently professed their love to us, yet the translation of this into consistent, supportive care may well have fallen short. If we can accept that there simply is no path to 'perfect' parenting, we can create space for questioning where we may have been mistreated, allowing for a clearer view of our own development.

Use the following multiple-choice questionnaire to see which option best reflects how you were parented while you were growing up.

1. **When you asked your parents 'Why?' about a rule or decision, they would usually answer**

a. 'Because I said so!'

b. With a calm explanation of their rationale, sometimes with open discussion.

c. With a vague 'Do whatever you want.'

d. Mostly no response – they were unavailable for questions.

2. **When you were naughty growing up**

a. You were often punished severely, sometimes without understanding why.

b. You were corrected, sometimes disciplined, but also guided on how to do better next time.

c. There was little structure or discipline – you were allowed to do whatever you wanted, without consequence.

d. Your parents were either absent or seemed oblivious to your actions.

3. **How involved were your parents in your daily activities?**

a. Strictly monitoring and controlling every aspect of your life.

b. Helpful and actively involved, while also allowing your autonomy.

c. Either uninvolved, leaving you to your own devices, or involved but feeling more like a friend than a parental figure.

d. Almost nonexistent; they neither knew nor cared about what you were up to.

4. **How would you describe your parents' affection towards you?**

a. Seldom given or conditional on your willingness to obey.

b. Consistent, warm and affirming.

c. Inconsistent, usually too much or too little.

d. Rare or nonexistent.

5. **When faced with challenges as a child**

a. You feared not living up to expectations and the possible consequences of this.

b. You were confident you could solve them, with guidance if necessary.

c. You often felt overwhelmed as you were unaccustomed to boundaries.

d. You felt very alone and insecure, with little to no support.

6. **Your parents' expectations of you as a child were**

a. Very high, with no margin for error.

b. High but reasonable, with tolerance for honest mistakes.

c. Almost never openly communicated. It was more like having peers than parents who set expectations for you.

d. It wasn't clear to you if they had any expectations at all.

Psychologist Diana Baumrind outlined three fundamental parenting styles in her research in the 1960s: authoritarian, authoritative and permissive. Stanford researchers Eleanor Maccoby and John Martin further enriched the theory in the 1980s by adding a fourth category: neglectful. Their collective model outlines the distinctive effects of different parenting approaches on child development, focusing on two crucial dimensions: *responsiveness* (how receptive and sensitive parents are to their children's needs) and *demandingness* (the degree of authority and expectations parents impose on their children).

Scoring your answers

Mostly As
Your upbringing seems to align with the authoritarian parenting style – an approach that leans heavily towards control. A common refrain in these households is a curt, 'Because I said so!' Questions are discouraged and boundaries are strict and closed to negotiation. Within such environments, children are powerless to express themselves and are conditioned to obey without question.

Though steeped in a desire for order, the implications of this parenting style can be manifold. Children may become perpetual followers, struggling to distinguish right from wrong, or harbouring a fragile self-esteem that depends on external affirmation. The irony lies in the fact that in spite of its rigidity and severity, authoritarian parenting may fail to impart meaningful values. When the overbearing presence fades, the formerly restrained child may rebel or fall prey to new kinds of manipulators.

Mostly Bs
Your upbringing aligns closely with the authoritative parenting style. Known for its balance between discipline and freedom, parents adopting this method establish clear boundaries and standards, while ensuring that their children feel nurtured – an approach widely termed as 'firm but fair'.

In such a setting, children are provided with an environment in which mistakes are viewed as opportunities for learning, and where guidance is at hand. These parents are reassuringly assertive without being overbearing. Their discipline leans towards support rather than punishment, aiming to raise children to be self-sufficient and socially conscious.

People who were raised under this kind of method typically develop a strong sense of self-worth, understand the value of responsibility, tackle problems wisely and have faith in their own choices.

Mostly Cs
The permissive parenting style seems to be most representative of your upbringing. Under this parental method, you may have experienced your parents as being more akin to your own peers or companions. Their discomfort around any show of disappointment on your part compelled them to immediately acquiesce to your desires.

It is a well-meaning approach, born, perhaps, from memories of their own childhood lived under an authoritarian iron fist. There is a certain dignity in responding to a child's needs with such empathy. Yet, without structure or limits, this style can cast a long shadow on the future. The result is either a child who is indignant about the actual conditions of life, or one who is deeply anxious due to a lack of guidance – a spectrum in which, at both ends, there is a struggle with self-regulation, a defiance when one's wishes are not immediately satisfied or a hasty retreat whenever one is faced with adversity.

Mostly Ds

Your experiences might correspond with the neglectful parenting style. Such parents are conspicuous in their absence, both physically and emotionally. Children in such environments wander about almost like orphans within their own homes, devoid of rules, structure or parental nurturing.

Here, parents' attitudes verge on a profound disinterest in the child's activities, an apparent apathy towards their feelings and an aloofness that might, in its extreme, imperil the child's safety, at times calling for their removal from such conditions.

The consequences of such parenting reverberate deeply. In later life, these individuals may face periods of depression, struggle to form close attachments, have a series of strained and unstable relationships, experience eruptions of rage and resentment and,

regrettably, feel an urge to withdraw into a shell, away from a world that feels so uninviting.

Reflective questions

What might have been the motives and fears behind your parents' actions?

Some parenting styles span generations, while others are deliberate departures from what came before. Based on your own upbringing, which patterns would you ideally emulate, and which do you feel compelled to break?

If your childhood were a novel, what lessons would it impart to its readers?

What is the most generous interpretation you can offer for the behaviour of your parents?

18. Family Roles

Psychologists Murray Bowen and Salvador Minuchin proposed that we tend to adopt particular roles as a way of handling the challenges of our families. We may be peacemakers, rebels, voices of conscience and so on.

The following test determines which predominant role you may have adopted to cope with the stresses of your family of origin:

1. When faced with family problems, my instinct is to

a. take on others' problems and responsibilities

b. ensure that everything appears fine and normal from the outside

c. 'act out' or sweep the hidden issues out from under the rug

d. stay well out of the way and withdraw

e. lighten the mood with humour or antics

2. My adult relationships tend to be

a. based on what I can materially or practically provide the other person

b. centred around being an emotionally stable presence for my partner and not 'rocking the boat'

c. confrontational and, admittedly, a little shallow at times

d. limited or distant; I avoid intimacy and much prefer being left alone

e. centred on pleasing the other person and keeping things 'nice' and amiable

3. What is your main sense of responsibility in your family?

a. Without me, the family would not survive.

b. I must always be seen as brave and strong to protect the family's reputation.

c. I challenge and question everything, even if it gets me into trouble.

d. As much as possible, I shun responsibilities and keep my distance from others.

e. I tend to joke about responsibilities or not bother with them.

4. When it comes to expressing emotions in my family

a. I put others' needs first and refrain from expressing my own feelings.

b. No matter what I feel inside, the main focus is to appear confident and in control for the sake of the family's reputation.

c. Even if it leads to confrontation or further problems, I will express my emotions freely.

d. I don't bother showing how I feel; I am doubtful anyone would pay any mind.

e. I try to lighten emotional moments with jokes to deflect from the real issues.

5. When family members criticise me, my first priority is to

a. make my best efforts to improve or fix the issue

b. keep my composure and be sure to hide any hurt feelings

c. criticise back, even if it causes conflict

d. withdraw or disregard the criticism. There's no point in doing more

e. make a joke out of it, no matter how much it affects me

6. When issues come up at work

a. I take on extra responsibilities, feeling the need to keep things going, and shield my colleagues from the consequences.

b. I strive for perfection and achievement, and take charge in ensuring we keep up appearances.

c. I challenge or confront things directly, sometimes drawing attention to myself and escalating the problem.

d. I keep my head down and wait for things to settle down.

e. I stay busy and use humour or light-heartedness to diffuse tension.

Scoring your answers

Mostly As: the Caretaker

The Caretaker feels an overwhelming responsibility to keep the family functioning. A child might become the surrogate parent, grounding their entire sense of self in how they can help and provide for others. In their eyes, without them, the family would simply fall apart. Unfortunately, often in their desperate attempt to keep crisis at bay, the Caretaker disrupts the potentially remedial process that a crisis can facilitate; their interference may actually prevent other family members from facing their issues and breaking their cycles of dysfunction.

Mostly Bs: the Hero

Often perfectionists, Heroes present as overachieving, resilient and optimistic. They might be known as go-getters, admired and rewarded for their bravery and strength. Their parents may view them as living proof of their own good parenting – after all, how could anyone believe a child this wonderful ever experienced hardship? Yet on the inside there is a risk of crumbling. From a young age, the Hero has learnt that expressing their true struggles would burden others; they therefore suffer in silence and may fall prey to stress-induced sickness and obsessive hard work. Their experiences have deprived them of a sense of the legitimate role of vulnerability in a good life.

Mostly Cs: the Scapegoat

Also known as 'the problem child', the Scapegoat prides themselves on being the truth-teller. They seek out the heart of the matter, refusing to let others sweep things under the rug. Through frequent problems at school, they often attract negative attention, which they believe is the best form of recognition they can get. The ultimate purpose of this role is a clever distraction from the real issues at hand. By drawing so much attention to their 'problem behaviours', and often becoming the 'identified patient' of the family, they masterfully hide the family's problems and, simultaneously, their own deeper vulnerabilities.

Mostly Ds: the Lost Child

The Lost Child, also known as 'the quiet one', adopts a strategy of avoidance when it comes to family issues. They seek privacy and solitude to escape the chaos, resulting in limited social interaction and difficulties with intimacy and solid relationships. By remaining small and quiet and seldom causing trouble, they allow parental figures to reassure themselves with the maxim, 'They seem OK, so things can't be too bad.' But inside, the Lost Child has ceased to believe in love and reassurance.

Mostly Es: the Mascot

The Mascot is the court jester of the family. Ready at any moment to break the tension and lighten the mood with mischievous jokes and antics, they can be relied upon to entertain and soothe other family members with their levity and silliness. They tend to become easily anxious when things are not in constant motion, and keep themselves busy wherever possible. They have been denied the chance to be appropriately serious by a family setting that is too close to tragedy.

The roles we adopt within our families are often ingenious responses to turbulent environments, helping us to contend with chaos and maintain a fragile equilibrium. But have these roles outlasted their necessity? How would it be if we were to step outside the confines of these roles? If we relinquished the need to be the fixer, the perfectionist, the truth-teller, the invisible one or the entertainer?

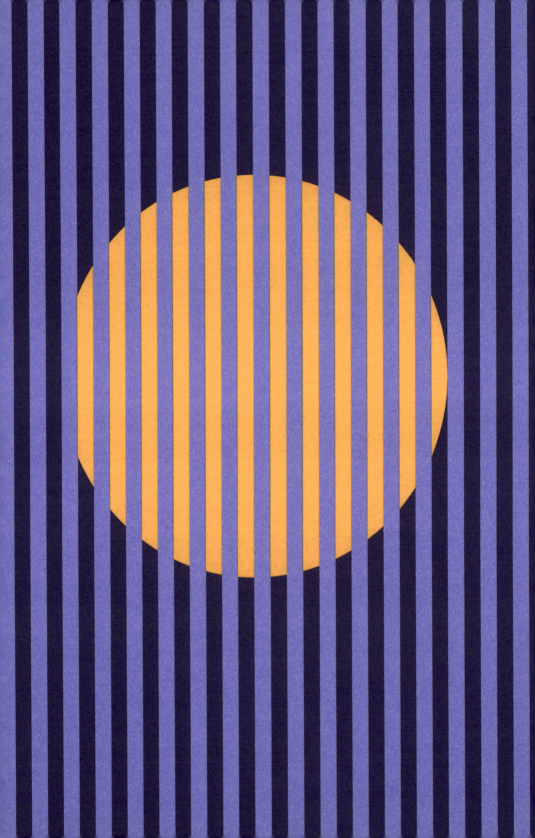

RELATIONSHIPS

19. The Letter-writing Test

A general principle of mental health is that the less we express, the more unwell we become. When we stifle rage, sadness or fear, we start to manifest secondary symptoms like sleeplessness, paranoia, bitterness and poor digestion. On the other hand, when we give voice to our pains, our spirits can lighten and our horizons can expand.

The obstacle many of us face is a lack of appropriate opportunities. We might be ready to express our feelings, but our external circumstances may not be conducive to doing so. The person we wish to address may already be deceased, or they might be too distracted, fragile or intimidating.

This situation might lead us erroneously to believe that there is no point in expressing our feelings. But it's essential to realise an intriguing aspect of our psyches: the importance lies less in ensuring the recipient hears our words and more in making sure we get a genuine chance to articulate our feelings. Expressing our emotions to an empty beach, a pillow or a chair can be as therapeutic as having a dialogue with a challenging relative or partner.

One of the best techniques for practising this principle is to write a letter we never intend to send, either because the recipient is no longer alive or because we doubt they would understand.

Begin your letter with 'Dear [recipient's name]' and end it with an appropriate sign-off. Take your time as you write, allowing your thoughts and feelings to flow naturally. Try not to worry too much about structure or perfection – this exercise is certainly not about crafting something polished.

The discipline of writing a long letter has the effect of galvanising our hitherto confused and disparate emotions, while forcing our intelligence to lay out our story in an emotionally logical way. As we write, we turn what might have been an inchoate sob into something intelligible, plausible, compassion-inducing and moving. We go from, 'I hate you so much' or, 'Why must you always ...' to a full recap of how we felt, why we suffered and what the legacy of our injury has been.

We can take our absent reader into the details of a story that they refused to see and may have done their best to silence. We are giving ourselves an opportunity to feel legitimate in our own eyes. We realise that the real audience we needed all along was ourselves.

20. The Conflict Resolution Exercise

We can perhaps only ever count on six to nine months of naturally conflict-free time in a long-term relationship with even the most delightful candidate; thereafter, what starts to count is whether a couple have the right conflict resolution techniques to hand – whether they know how to repair after a rupture.

It is during this transition from the 'honeymoon phase' to the realities of partnership that the strength of a relationship is truly put to the test. The key to enduring love is not the absence of conflict, but rather the ability to negotiate disagreements with sensitivity, tolerance and effective communication.

This is a matter of experience – and a good couple should accept that they probably don't already have it, and so should humbly recognise that they need some education. Lovers should regularly make room to ask themselves – in a calm spirit of gentle openness and curiosity – two ostensibly simple, yet hugely central and effective, questions:

What are you angry with me about?

How have I scared you recently?

To pull out of the negative spiral requires discipline and adherence to a basic three-stage process:

1. Share the fear behind the anger

All arguments come down to fear. They may seem to be about all sorts of things – from what happened to the phone charger to what is being cooked for dinner – but they inevitably come down to the same fear: that we are not properly loved and are therefore in danger.

It is essential to exchange the expression of anger for regular, brave revelations of the reasons why we are afraid. We need to swap global accusations ('You're a ...') for personal confessions of fear ('When you ... it makes me feel scared and unsafe').

2. **Explain the cause of the fear**

We then have to explain the reasons for our fear. We need to share a backstory – ideally with reference to something in our childhoods – about why we are especially sensitive over a specific topic: 'I'm scared of x because, a long time ago, my y was so z.' Our complaint shifts from sounding judgemental and stifling to sounding poignant and touching.

3. **Mutually apologise for the madness**

The other person must, in turn, immediately reveal their own fear that has been triggered by our complaint (they will have one too) and, along with it, the cause of their fear: 'When you accuse me of x, I feel afraid of y.' And then: 'This makes me afraid because ...'

Throughout, both people should accept that they are bringing a distorted, overly intense perspective to the situation. No one should lay claim to normality. Here are two complex and flawed people trying to make themselves understood. No one is perfect and no one is beyond understanding.

If couples follow this simple three-stage rule, there will still be arguments at points, but love will be more likely to survive and, as each person understands the other's vulnerabilities ever better, it will deepen and grow.

To help guide this process, consider the following sentence completion prompts:

I am angry with my partner about ...

My partner has scared me lately because ...

For me, this argument comes down to the fear that ...

When I accuse my partner of ..., it actually stems from my fear of ...

When my partner accuses me of ..., I feel afraid of ... because ...

During conflicts, I must remember that my perspective might be distorted because ...

21.   Should I Be with Them?

We expect to be deeply happy in love, and we therefore spend a good deal of time wondering whether our relationships are essentially normal in their sexual and psychological frustrations, or whether we are beset by unusually pathological patterns that should impel us to get out as soon as we can.

What films or novels we've been exposed to, the state of our friends' relationships, the degree of noise surrounding new, sexually driven dating apps, not to mention how much sleep we've had can all play humblingly large roles in influencing us one way or another.

The only thing determining whether to stay in or leave a relationship is how we feel, which can be a pretty hard matter indeed to work out for ourselves, since our feelings have a dispiriting habit of shifting and evading any efforts at rational qualification.

In the circumstances, it might help to have a set of questions – devil's advocate in nature – to fall back on; a kind of checklist to dialogue with in one's mind in the silent hours of the morning, from the chill vantage point of the bed in the spare room.

Please indicate whether you agree or disagree with each of the following statements based on your current relationship with your partner.

1. They know how to comfort me well in a crisis.

    Agree / Disagree

2. I feel they deeply care about my well-being and flourishing.

    Agree / Disagree

3. When I have something truly important to communicate to them, they listen.

    Agree / Disagree

4. They make an effort to change for me.

    Agree / Disagree

5. They are kind to the child in me.

    Agree / Disagree

6. I enjoy talking with them.

    Agree / Disagree

7. They have my back.

    Agree / Disagree

8. I feel heard by them.

Agree / Disagree

9. I feel they are on my side.

Agree / Disagree

10. I feel appreciated according to my own distinctive love language(s). (This might mean that they know I like to leave the kitchen a certain way, or that they take my views on social life or intimacy into account.)

Agree / Disagree

11. They know I am making an effort in their name.

Agree / Disagree

12. I feel wanted, emotionally and physically.

Agree / Disagree

13. Insofar as they are difficult to be around (and we all are), they explain why this is so. They tell me calmly and with grace how they are a little mad and, with reference to their past, why. They never insist proudly or defensively on their normality.

Agree / Disagree

14. They strive to remain calm around my most trying sides. They do not humiliate me about my flaws. My partner is an excellent teacher and diplomat of difficult messages.

Agree / Disagree

Scoring your answers

When you have completed the exercise, give 1 point for each 'Agree' response. Add up your total points out of 14.

12–14 points
The foundation of your relationship appears strong and solid. Communicate and nurture the relationship to ensure its ongoing health.

9–11 points
Your relationship shows promise, but there is room for improvement.

5–8 points
There may be some obstacles in your relationship that can be addressed through open dialogue.

1–4 points
Your relationship may be facing some pressing issues that require immediate attention or help from a relationship therapist.

22.

Radically Honest Dating

Normally, dates are about trying to show how marvellous we are. Here, we suggest a practice called 'radically honest dating'. The exercise goes like this:

1. Two people sit together in a café or restaurant.

2. Person A says something very honest about how *difficult* they are to be with in a relationship.

3. Person B listens but says nothing. Then they respond with something equally honest about how difficult they are to be with.

4. They repeat this ten times – back and forth.

Example

Person A	Person B
I get incredibly anxious if someone doesn't text back within an hour. I'll check my phone about fifty times.	I deliberately push people away when they start getting too close. I've ended three relationships right when they were getting serious.
I'm still obsessed with my ex from five years ago. I compare everyone to them.	I pretend to be really independent, but actually I'm terrified of being alone.
I need constant reassurance that I'm attractive. It drives partners crazy, but I can't stop asking.	I've never told anyone how I really feel. I always say I'm fine even when I'm falling apart.

I get jealous when my partner has fun without me. I try to make them feel guilty about it.

I test people by creating small crises to see if they'll stick around.

I sabotage relationships when they're going well because I don't think I deserve happiness.

I'm so afraid of conflict that I'll agree to anything, then get resentful later.

I judge potential partners on ridiculous superficial criteria because I'm scared of real connection.

I pick fights when I'm feeling vulnerable because anger feels safer than fear.

Sometimes I pretend to be asleep just to avoid having to talk about feelings.

I use work as an excuse to avoid intimacy. I'll stay late at the office when things get emotional.

I become whatever I think the other person wants. I don't even know who I really am any more.

I need to control everything in the relationship. The uncertainty of letting go terrifies me.

I can't bear physical affection unless I'm drunk. I stiffen up when someone tries to hug me.

I tell everyone about our private problems. I can't keep anything to myself.

I've never had a relationship last longer than six months. I always find a reason to leave.

I act like I don't care about anyone, but really I care too much about everyone.

By the end of many rounds of this, two people may not idealise one another, but they stand to achieve something far more useful and interesting: understanding, compassion and (perhaps) even deeply liking one another.

23. Attachment Questionnaire

One of the greatest questionnaires in the history of 20th-century psychology had a modest start in the pages of a local Colorado newspaper, *The Rocky Mountain News*, in July 1985. The work of two University of Denver psychologists, Cindy Hazan and Phillip Shaver, the questionnaire asked readers to identify which of three statements most closely reflected who they are in love.

To hugely improve our chances of thriving in relationships, we should dare to take the same test:

A. I find it relatively easy to get close to others and am comfortable depending on them and having them depend on me. I don't worry about being abandoned or about someone getting too close to me.

B. I find that others are reluctant to get as close as I would like. I often worry that my partner doesn't really love me or won't want to stay with me. I want to get very close to my partner, and this sometimes scares people away.

C. I am somewhat uncomfortable being close to others; I find it difficult to trust them completely, difficult to allow myself to depend on them. I am nervous when anyone gets too close, and often, others want me to be more intimate than I feel comfortable being.

The options refer to the three main styles of relating to others, which were first identified by the English psychologist John Bowlby, the inventor of attachment theory, in the 1950s and 1960s.

Option A signals what is known as the *secure* pattern of attachment, whereby love and trust come easily.

Option B refers to the *anxious* pattern of attachment, whereby one longs to be intimate with others but is continuously scared of being let down and often precipitates crises in relationships through counter-productively aggressive behaviour.

Option C is what is known as the *avoidant* pattern of attachment, whereby it feels much easier to avoid the dangers of intimacy through solitary activities and emotional withdrawal.

Questionnaires in newspapers are rarely of much use, but Hazan and Shaver's is the momentous exception. If there is one thing we should do to improve our relationships, it is to know which of the three categories we predominantly belong to – and to deploy that knowledge in love, so as to warn ourselves and others of the traps we might fall into.

We then need a little training, because at least half of us are not secure in love; we belong in the camps of either the avoidant or the anxious, and we have – to complicate matters – an above-average propensity to fall in love with someone from the other damaged side, thereby aggravating our insecurities and defences in the process.

If you don't immediately identify with one of the three categories, the following questionnaire could help you to identify which attachment style you have.

1. By chance, you meet someone attractive in a bookshop and exchange a few pleasant (but not very consequential) remarks. They leave by saying, 'See you around.' What are you most likely to do next?

a. Nothing. They'll have a partner anyway.

b. Try to track them down on social media and return to the shop in the hope of bumping into them again.

c. Not too much. They seemed nice enough, but so do lots of people. Perhaps I'll meet them again, who knows!

2. You arrange to go on a date with a charming stranger who you met at the gym, and you have a very enjoyable time. When it's time to part, what do you do?

a. Nothing at all; wait to see if they call you.

b. Fix a date in your diary for meeting up a second time.

c. Tell them you had a lovely time – smile warmly.

3. Your partner of five years says they will be home to enjoy the dinner you've cooked for them at 7 p.m. It is now 7.15 p.m. and you haven't heard anything from them. The dinner is going cold. What do you do?

a. Start eating. Why bother waiting for someone who can't keep their promises?

b. Start calling them repeatedly. You can't help thinking that something terrible might have happened to them.

c. Sit tight. It's not ideal, but the delay isn't massive and there will most likely be an explanation in due course.

4. An old friend has borrowed £50 from you and is late paying it back. What do you do?

a. Grit your teeth but say nothing and remind yourself not to be so generous in future.

b. Call them and demand the money back as soon as possible. You don't want people taking advantage of you – even old friends.

c. Call them and explain that the money is important to you and it would be great if they could return it to you in the next few days.

5. At a dinner party, your partner makes an unkind joke about your choice of outfit in front of all of your friends. What do you do?

a. Say nothing and sulk on the way home.

b. Have a huge argument in the car on the way home.

c. Wait until the two of you are alone together and explain carefully why the joke upset you.

6. As you lie awake in the early hours, you go to check the time on your partner's phone and inadvertently discover a text from one of their exes saying how much they enjoyed catching up over a drink together the other night. What do you do?

a. Arrange a drink with one of your own exes to see how your partner responds.

b. Wake them up immediately and demand to know what's going on between the two of them.

b. Go back to sleep. They remain friends, and you can trust that their relationship doesn't go any further than that. But you will ask a question or two gently as well. Why not?

7. In the early weeks of a new relationship, your partner sends you a message that ends with the words 'I love you'. What do you do?

a. Freeze. You don't want to give them the wrong impression, and the whole thing feels intense.

b. Say it back. And add a few extra kisses.

c. Check in with how you feel. If you're unsure, say how touched you were, but say you need a little more time before you can honestly return the sentiment – but that you are heading in that direction.

8. Eight months into your relationship, you realise you and your partner have gone a whole week without having sex. How do you feel?

a. Resigned. A gradual waning of physical attraction and sexual chemistry is inevitable in most relationships. Say nothing.

b. Accuse them of no longer finding you attractive.

c. Ask them how they feel about the gap and explain your sense of it.

9. Imagine you are a 10-year-old child and your mother is an hour late to collect you from football practice, leaving you sitting alone on the curb in the winter cold. When she finally arrives, what do you do?

a. Sulk and refuse to speak to her all the way home.

b. Cling to her legs until she promises never to be late again.

c. Forgive her, providing she sincerely apologises.

10. Which of the following is the most accurate description of the phrase 'true love'?

a. A beguiling but ultimately dangerous fiction.

b. A beautiful idea and the ultimate goal of one's romantic life.

c. A beautiful, sometimes difficult, sometimes amazing, ambition.

Scoring your answers

Mostly As: avoidant attachment

From an early age, you have probably known quite a few let-downs. But you aren't one to whimper. You present a rather stoic face to the world. If someone lets you down, you are concerned to maintain a dignified facade. You tend not to tell people who've disappointed you: what would be the point? You like to be on your own a lot, especially when things go wrong. It can feel safer that way. Quite a few things probably weren't ideal in childhood. You learnt to cope – perhaps a bit too well. Trust doesn't come easily, strength does.

It can be very hard to change your attachment style, but knowing which one you might have is a vital first step. You might want to start to observe how you quickly shut down when your partner has disappointed you – and how your characteristic response to hurt is not to feel. Consider that your independence includes, somewhere, an element of fear. Having a vocabulary with which to discuss our patterns of love can be very helpful. Next time you feel like being completely alone and insist that your partner (who might have hurt you a little emotionally) means nothing to you, think of the concept of avoidance.

Mostly Bs: anxious attachment

You long to be close to people, very close, but often find the reality disappointing. You feel intensely but are frequently let down. Sometimes you get very angry with people in whom you'd invested a lot. The love you knew in childhood was warm but perhaps erratic. Probably people let you down. It's made your emotional needs feel urgent and powerful and your sense of emotional stability slightly rocky. You frequently feel that those you love are slipping away from you.

It can be very hard to change your attachment style, but knowing which one you might have is a vital first step. You might want to start to observe how nervous you can feel about your partner's intentions – sometimes a bit unfairly. You could try to explain that you've done a questionnaire, that the answer was 'anxious' and that this interests you rather a lot. Having a vocabulary with which to discuss our patterns of love can be very helpful. Next time you feel abandoned or humiliated, take a moment to ask whether bad intentions are really at play.

Mostly Cs: secure attachment

You've enjoyed a relatively stable and reliable childhood and are used to communicating your needs clearly, with a good expectation of being heard at least some of the time. You have faith that upsets can generally be corrected if they're sensibly discussed. When people let you down, it doesn't darken your faith in humanity as a whole, or indeed in yourself. These things happen. You're happy being on your own, but even happier being with someone you love. You've had some very satisfying relationships in the past. You like your parents and they like you.

You stand a chance of being very happy in your relationships; everything won't always go right, but you have the psychological tools to cope when they don't.

24. Communication Questionnaire

It is often said that one of the most vital indicators of success in relationships is the ability to communicate well. But in order to do this, we first need to understand the level of skill we currently possess. This questionnaire aims to help us assess our current capacities for communication – and then gently point us towards areas of improvement.

1. A lot of psychology is mere babble. I'm pretty sceptical about this kind of exercise.

   True / False

2. Pretty often, talking a problem over with someone makes it worse.

   True / False

3. Most people never fundamentally change.

   True / False

4. It's sad but only too normal to feel very alone.

   True / False

5. I often get into sulks.

   True / False

6. When a partner upsets me, I like to tell them right away.

   True / False

7. When I'm properly upset, I often say nothing.

   True / False

8. If someone really loves you, they should understand many things about you without the need to spell them out.

   True / False

9. When something matters a lot to me, and someone is being obtuse, it can be hard to stay calm.

   True / False

10. Most people are not quite to be trusted.

    True / False

11. Sometimes, shouting at someone can get them to appreciate a point.

True / False

12. I'm good at arguing.

True / False

13. Having a lot of heavy discussions with a partner is an indicator that the relationship is not going well.

True / False

14. I'm generally pretty good at guessing what's in other people's minds.

True / False

15. As a child, my parents were very interested in listening to what I had to say.

True / False

16. I saw my parents communicate their frustrations with one another with maturity and good humour.

True / False

17. I've been able to tell my parents very clearly how I feel about them and my childhood.

True / False

18. I'd never tell my partner the true range of my sexual interests.

True / False

19. You can teach anyone anything really, if you put enough work into it.

True / False

20. I'm pretty despairing of most human beings.

True / False

Scoring your answers

Use the scoring system below to add up your answers to the questions.

For statements 1, 2, 3, 5, 7, 8, 9, 10, 11, 12, 13, 14, 18 and 20:

True = 0 points   False = 1 point

For statements 4, 6, 15, 16, 17 and 19:

True = 1 point   False = 0 points

0–6: a pretty poor communicator

Good communication is extremely difficult – and it certainly doesn't come naturally to most of us. If we have difficulties communicating, it is likely because no one communicated especially well around us in our early years. There was likely to have been a lot of anger, suppressed rage and 'acting out'.

It isn't our fault that we're not gifted communicators – but there's a huge amount we can do to improve our normal patterns. We can, first and foremost, learn the art of vulnerable disclosure. We can say what is truly ailing us and dare to believe that we can be heard, so long as we speak calmly and without recrimination. We can put aside our defences and our temptations to get angry, to blame or to slam the door and walk out. Instead, we can carefully and generously delineate why we are disappointed and how we would like others to understand us.

Most of what makes us poor communicators is fear. It's fear that makes us rush, that makes us shout, that makes us say nothing. This suggests that what can best improve communication is love: a tender attitude towards ourselves that gives us a chance to say what we really mean and to hope that, this time, someone we care about will understand. We all have the opportunity to become the good communicators we would, deep down, love to be.

7–20: a good communicator

You can congratulate yourself and thank those who helped you to grow into the good communicator you are today. You recognise that communication is the essence of healthy, lasting relationships. You don't expect your partner to understand what's bothering you unless you spell it out for them. You don't fear arguments (which are preferable to silence) and accept that having frequent and often heavy discussions with your partner is a sign of the strength of a relationship, not a reflection of its weakness.

You probably learnt how to communicate from your parents, who encouraged you to vocalise and discuss your feelings from an early age; they have done you an enormous service. Above all, you understand that the role of a lover is to be – at points – a teacher: helping a partner to understand your flaws as you understand theirs, so that the relationship ends up as a mutual exploration of one another's complicated realities.

25. | Connection Prompts

We tend to chat with our partners all the time, but often not about what really counts – the sorts of topics that clear the air, that reintroduce a spirit of fun, that draw us together, or that make us remember what is really special about being part of a couple.

Here is a series of questions and sentence stubs to help couples rekindle affection. They lead naturally to chats about what we are ready to forgive, what we deeply appreciate, what remains exciting and what is especially worth cherishing.

Appreciation

What do you really admire about your partner?

When do you feel tenderly towards your partner?

Describe a time when you were in particular difficulties and felt especially helped and looked after by your partner.

I think that my partner is at their most endearing when …

They touch my heart when …

Aspiration

What do you want more of in your life in the time that remains?

What could you celebrate more in your relationship?

What do you look forward to in your future together?

Guess what your partner thinks is the meaning of their life. Did you get it right?

Ask your partner how they think you could make your relationship more surprising.

Desire

Remember a particularly erotic time. Where were you, what happened and how did it feel?

How would you like to come back together again at the end of every day? Describe it in detail.

Name three parts of the other person's body and face that you especially like.

I'd love my partner to give me a bit more confidence sexually around …

What I don't tell my partner often enough is …

Forgiveness

For which of your flaws would you like to be forgiven?

How have you let your partner down?

How could you do better?

If I could go back in time in our relationship, I'd love to change how I ...

The trick to understanding why I can sometimes be difficult is to remember that ...

Growth

If I had known my partner in childhood, I might have loved to ...

I pledge to work on my ...

What I'd love to change about myself is ...

How have you changed over the past few years?

Ten years from now, how would you like to have changed?

What did you learn?

Connection and closeness can (strangely but truly) be generated almost on demand by the right sort of conversations.

26. The Boundaries Test

One of the reasons why our lives might be less fulfilling than they should be is that we have missed out on the critical art of laying down boundaries. Laying down boundaries involves informing those around us of a given set of objectively reasonable things that we require in order to feel respected and happy, while doing so in a way that conveys confidence, self-possession, kindness and strength.

Those who can successfully lay down boundaries will tell their child that though they love them very much, once this game is over it will be time to go to bed, and crying or kicking won't make any difference. The good boundary-builder will wait until everyone is well-rested to tell their partner that, though they usually love them taking initiative, when it comes to their own family, they want to be left in charge – and therefore don't want the partner to call up their mother-in-law without warning in order to arrange the forthcoming holidays. At work, the boundaried manager will tell their new hire that though they want to be supportive where possible, it simply isn't their role to manage budgets for others.

However, because most of us have not been educated in this byway of emotional maturity, the boundaries are either nonexistent or else get thrown up in a jerky and destructive manner. As the technical language has it, we are either too *compliant* or too *rigid*. In a relationship, we might never explain what we require in order to feel content, and therefore either store up our resentments or burst into unexplained rages that exhaust our partner's capacity for love. At work, we might develop a reputation as a pushover or an unreasonable tyrant.

Invariably, those who can't lay down boundaries have not, in their early lives, had their own boundaries respected. Someone didn't allow them to say when they were unhappy with a genuinely difficult situation, or they insinuated that being good meant falling in line. No one modelled the skill of winning, graceful objection. And so, now, when the time comes to make a request of others, they are faced with three powerful anxieties:

If I speak up, they will hate me.

If I speak up, I will become a target for retribution.

If I speak up, I will feel like a horrible person.

Though such fears manifest themselves as unquestionable certainties, they are amenable to gentle probing. People almost never hate those who make polite and reasonably framed demands; in fact, they tend to respect and like them a little more.

An alternative response to building boundaries is a habit of throwing up walls topped with razor wire or, to put it more colloquially, a tendency to get swiftly defensive. The manically defensive person will assume that:

Everyone is trying to hurt them badly.

No one will listen unless they hit back with immense force.

Their needs cannot ever truly be met.

Yet the alternative to lacking all boundaries is not violent defensiveness. There is always a means to make a sound case without reaching for a weapon.

Complete the table below to garner a sense of how boundaries were modelled for you as a child. Give each statement a score out of 10.

My parent ...	Score out of 10
modelled respectful and reasonable expectations	
expressed their needs confidently, without aggression	
allowed me to voice discomfort in challenging situations	
emphasised the importance of self-respect	

showed how to manage disagreements
gracefully

....

supported self-possession without fear
of retribution

....

was emotionally resilient without
defensive walls

....

respected my individuality and
personal boundaries

....

encouraged assertiveness without hostility

....

demonstrated clear, respectful communication

....

valued my input in decisions

....

modelled healthy self-expression

....

Complete the following sentences to deepen your understanding of
your childhood experiences:

In childhood

....

Growing up, the messages I received about setting
boundaries were ...

....

A time I tried to set a boundary was ... How others responded was ...

....

When I tried to set a boundary ...

....

If I spoke up, people would ...

....

When I expressed my needs as a child, it often resulted in ...

....

The way boundaries were modelled looked like ...

....

The fears I had around setting boundaries included ...

The lessons I took from my childhood about asserting
boundaries were …

Building on this, complete the following sentences to explore how you
currently manage boundaries in adult relationships:

In relationships

When boundaries are crossed in my current relationship, I tend to …

A time I tried to set a boundary was … How others responded was …

If I speak up …

In intimate relationships, I find it most challenging to …
regarding boundaries.

My partner often reacts … to my boundaries.

The one thing I wish my partner understood about my
boundaries is …

In my past relationships, a common boundary issue was …

When it comes to boundaries, I often feel most secure when …

When it comes to boundaries, I often feel most insecure when …

The process of boundary-setting is not instinctual for many of us;
rather, it is a skill that requires enormous practice. Studying how
boundaries were handled by our early caregivers makes visible the
subconscious beliefs that could be driving our adult interactions.
Confronting the outdated fears and anxieties we associate with setting
boundaries is crucial to redefining them. It enables us to address
issues rationally and to stop equating our self-worth with unwavering
compliance or, conversely, with stern or angry defensiveness.

27. The Defensiveness Test

However sweet and fascinating two people might initially be, it is inescapable that they will also, with time and the birth of true intimacy, stumble upon aspects of one another's characters that cannot help but generate difficulties and a degree of dismay.

Each partner could be determined to be only kind, but the way that they boil an egg, do the household chores, deal with their suitcase on returning from a trip, handle the house keys or tell an anecdote will gradually unleash powerful degrees of frustration or puzzlement in those who have to share their lives.

The problem starts when we, as partners, venture to air our responses. Our partner might get angry or sad, but the underlying message is the same: being found in some way imperfect is entirely unacceptable and deeply contrary to the spirit of true love.

Consider the following scenarios and select the response that best captures your feelings and communication style in each situation. Remember, while we strive to address issues with grace and dignity, we can sometimes fall into the trap of reacting with childish impudence. Let's explore how you might handle these everyday challenges with a touch of honesty.

1. After a long day at work, you come home to find the sink full of dirty dishes. Your partner is relaxing on the sofa, watching television. What do you say?

a. 'The kitchen is a tip. What is wrong with you?'

b. 'Why should I have to clean up after you? You can't blame me for shouting, I've had a terrible day!'

c. 'You're "tired"? Cry me a river. I've been working hard all day and all you do when you come home from work is flop down on that sofa like a child and watch stupid TV shows. Could you be any more pathetic?'

d. Nothing. Clearly upset, you clean the entire kitchen yourself with a heavy sigh.

2. Your partner failed to remind you about a concert you were both looking forward to attending. Now the date has passed and the expensive tickets are non-refundable. What do you say?

a. 'You always do this! It's no surprise, you're so irresponsible.'

b. 'Why is it always on me to remember? You could've set a reminder too!'

c. 'Here we go again, money down the drain. It's astounding how someone as inept as you can function at all.'

d. Instead of discussing it further, you go cold and avoid talking to your partner for the rest of the evening.

3. After going through your monthly finances, you realise you've spent more than you budgeted. This month you know you purchased some extra items, but your partner also incurred some unplanned expenses. What do you say?

a. 'You always overspend, you're so selfish! You never think of me!'

b. 'This is clearly all your fault. I only ever spend on essentials.'

c. 'If you didn't act like money grows on trees, we wouldn't be having this issue.'

d. You shut down, unwilling to discuss further.

4. You and your partner are planning a holiday. You've done most of the research and your partner isn't helping. What do you say?

a. 'You never contribute to planning! How can you be so lazy?'

b. 'Don't blame me if I end up making all the decisions. It's not like I have a choice when no one else steps up.'

c. 'Must be great sitting back while I do all the work. You seem to believe your time is more precious than mine.'

d. You continue planning without involving them, feeling deeply frustrated but saying nothing.

Scoring your answers

This is where the categories identified by Dr John Gottman in his model of the 'Four Horsemen'– that is, the strongest indicators that a relationship will break down – become instrumental.

Mostly As: criticism

With harsh blame and hurtful expressions of judgement and disapproval, we criticise our partner's perceived personal flaws. When they make a mistake, we target their inherent worth, telling them: 'You never do anything right!' When they don't share household chores, we accuse them of being 'lazy' and 'ungrateful'. When they struggle to get along with our friends, we berate them for their awkwardness.

To move past this destructive behaviour, we must confront the painful possibility that our harsh words likely stem from our own insecurities. Hurling criticism at our partners allows us to project our insecurities outward. If, for instance, we find ourselves continually criticising their social skills, or lack thereof, it may be worth exploring our own social insecurities.

We go beyond criticism when we shift our focus from personal attacks to addressing behaviours that can change, or implementing a constructive solution. Instead of accusing our partner of being 'lazy', we might say, 'Let's set up a routine for sharing household chores.'

With all that said, if you and your partner are critical of each other, there is no need to assume that your relationship is doomed to fail. The trouble with criticism is that, once it becomes pervasive, it lays the path for the other, far deadlier horsemen to follow.

Mostly Bs: defensiveness

Behind defensiveness there is always a dread of being humiliated and abandoned. But a decent partner, if we let them know what we're afraid of, will be moved by our tender desperation and hasty fear. They should help us to see that it is not criticism, but an inability to accept its gentle manifestations with grace, that is the problem. If love really required an absence of even the most minor flaws, no one could possibly qualify for a relationship.

We will move past defensiveness when every nagging insecurity that we had previously banished to the periphery of consciousness has been pulled squarely into the centre and there examined and defused. We should consider every harrowing possibility:

that we are indeed a poor friend, a dismal worker, a narrow-minded traveller and overall a thoroughly shortsighted and dim-witted human. Thereafter, we might hear much that is negative, but we'll never need to bite in response to a remark, because either it will be false, and therefore can be discarded without fluster, or it will be true, and we'll be able to remain even-tempered because we'll be as aware as our angriest opponent of its justice and validity. We'll know who we are – and so will never need to greet a challenging idea about us with weapons again.

Mostly Cs: contempt

Similarly to criticism, it is easier to belittle others than to admit our own fears of inadequacy. With an embittered, sarcastic tone, we want our partners to feel our spite and disgust – a behaviour likely stemming from long-standing, festering disappointment. Beneath this guise lies a deeply sorrowful, dejected and wounded core.

Our contempt acts as a guard against the fear of being inadequate and unloved. It is a mechanism of defence that keeps us from facing our own vulnerabilities. By displaying contempt, we temporarily elevate ourselves above others, masking the deep-seated fears that we are too frightened to address. To move past contempt, we must bring our insecurities to the forefront, examine them and disarm them.

We should consider our responses. When our partner forgets once again to load the dishwasher, we may be tempted by our own acrimony to spite them: 'Are you really so forgetful?' we might say with an eye roll. With a more constructive approach, we can take a sharp inhale and say, 'I understand that you've been busy lately, but could you please remember to load the dishwasher when I work late? I'd appreciate it.' This method avoids moral superiority and casting blame in favour of co-operation, diffusing tension with a joint solution.

Mostly Ds: stonewalling

When we stonewall, we retreat behind an impenetrable fortress of silence and emotional withdrawal, isolating ourselves from our partners, with profound consequences. Rather than confronting the issues directly, we make evasive efforts: tuning out, turning away, acting busy or engaging in obsessive or distracting behaviours. This stifles resolution, leaving conflicts unresolved and emotions unaddressed. The silent treatment can be interpreted as a lack of care or concern, only fuelling resentment and deepening the divide between partners. Over time, this pattern can erode the very foundation of trust and intimacy that the relationship was originally built upon.

By refusing to engage, we temporarily protect ourselves from the anxiety and discomfort associated with vulnerable and honest communication. However, this avoidance only exacerbates the underlying issues, leading to a cycle of frustration and alienation. The person who stonewalls may feel a temporary sense of relief, but their partner is left feeling unheard, unimportant and disconnected.

At its centre, stonewalling is a defence mechanism stemming from a deep-seated fear of conflict and a sense of being overwhelmed or powerless in the face of emotional confrontation. To move beyond stonewalling, it is crucial to recognise our triggers for shutting down. By bringing our vulnerabilities to light, we can start to address them constructively. This involves facing our fears of inadequacy and rejection head on in personal reflection.

Changing our responses to conflict is key to every relationship's survival. 'Love me for who I am' is the fateful rallying cry of all lovers headed for disaster; it is, in reality, a monstrously unfair demand to be loved just as we are, given our panoply of faults, compulsions and immaturities. With a modicum of self-awareness and honesty, we should only ever expect to be loved for who we hope to be, for who we are at our best moments, for the good that is in us in a latent and yet unrealised state.

The spirit of true love should require that whenever there is feedback, we turn gratefully to our partner and ask for more, that we continuously search to access a better version of ourselves, that we see love as a classroom in which our lover can teach us one or two things about who we should become – rather than a burrow in which our existing errors can be endorsed and ratified.

In reality, we are love-worthy not because we are perfect, but because none of us ever can be.

28. A Fear of Intimacy Test

Imagine you are in a relationship in which you appreciate your partner in a host of ways, but at the same time wonder – perhaps with increasing intensity – whether or not you should continue to be with them. Such doubts might indicate that you should leave the relationship, but that would be to miss a painful nuance that is likely to nag strongly at the conscience of any moderately informed, psychologically aware person: Am I really not so keen, or might I simply have a fear of intimacy? Is my desire to end things evidence of disinterest or – paradoxically – proof that my interest is too intense and therefore threatening my sense of integrity, triggering a wish to flee?

That we should find ourselves ruminating in this way is a legacy of pioneering work carried out in the 20th century by psychotherapists including John Bowlby, Erich Fromm, George R. Bach, David Shulman and Leslie Greenberg, who in slightly different ways all posited the theory that humans are under the sway of two diametrically opposed inclinations: to seek closeness with others on the one hand and to escape from them for fear of let-down on the other – the latter generally created by an actual experience of let-down during a childhood that has not been sufficiently explored or understood.

The theory places us at the sharp end of the dilemmas of self-knowledge. We might be sitting across the table from someone at dinner, with a strong impression that we'd be better off with another candidate, and at the same time, outside of conscious awareness, be thinking in this way only because it is our companion's rightness that is gnawing at our walled-off, emotionally reticent and wounded character.

How might we learn to separate a legitimate aversion for someone from an inhibition about intimacy? We might start by asking ourselves some of the following questions:

1. **Complete the sentence: *If someone knew me completely, they would think I was ...***

Some of what may lie behind our desire to get out of a relationship as it deepens is an unease about being known. The more someone sees who we are, the more they might take fright at what they discover. A fear of intimacy can, in essence, come down to a belief in our fundamental unacceptability.

2. **Which of the following seems most immediately true: 'people can be trusted' or 'people let you down'?**

We don't want to stick around, not because we dislike our partner so much, but because nothing in our pasts suggests to us that people in general are capable of extensive loyalty or kindness. It isn't the partner's sweetness that is alarming us, so much as our unconscious trepidation about when it might end, as our histories suggest it always will.

3. **In life in general, how easy do you find it to be happy?**

Our love stories should be considered alongside our broader capacities for contentment – the extent to which we can derive pleasure from any experience, be it a holiday, a gift, money or visible success. Being content in any way may alarm us because it might once have triggered the jealousy or sadness of an angry or fragile parent. We may find it easier to fail than to be threatened because we have won.

4. **When did this desire to leave your partner set in? Did you ever feel keen about them – or did your coldness descend principally once they decided they felt warmly for you?**

It pays to look closely at chronology and explore whether the nauseous feeling arose recently or was there from the start. The real issue may not have anything to do with a dislike of the partner overall. We may just not be able to forgive them for one specific lapse: that they have had the bad taste to approve of someone like us. We could start to respect them once more if only they would come to their senses and better align their view of us with our view of ourselves. The issue may be self-hatred – not hatred or disinterest per se.

5. Did your parents offer their love freely or were they – in a variety of ways – a bit of a challenge?

Adult love sits upon a base formed in childhood, and our pasts may have taught us that the really interesting, special people are those who are not generally available, don't warmly approve and always mix their affection with judgement and aloofness. The principal mistake of a current partner might be that they aren't following the script of pain we have been habituated to expect. They don't have the tricky personalities of those we grew up to admire. They are entirely alien – and therefore daunting – in their steady kindness.

The theory of the fear of intimacy has hugely enriched our analyses of what may be at play in love. Optimistically, it has given us a handy way of framing a problem for which we should be understood rather than condemned. We can now explain to our partners that we have something poignant to confess: that we don't truly want to run away, we're just wrestling with a very powerful but unreliable itch to escape an unfamiliar, unwarranted feeling of being accepted.

29. A Job Spec for Love

Few things could sound as offensive and unromantic as to draw comparisons between hiring an employee and getting together with a partner. We're highly attuned to the many differences between commercial recruitment and love: money plays an overt role in the first, ideally rather little in the second. One is about cold objectives and annual targets, the other about feelings and tenderness.

But we can end up emphasising the differences at our cost. An unhelpful nebulousness can afflict our search for love. We can fall prey to notions that it would be vulgar or unseemly to think directly about how to accomplish our ends; that we must trust in fate and keep things 'old-fashioned'. We may imagine that if someone was truly meant to be with us, they would – paradoxically – arrive in our lives with minimal intent on our part (the less we have to do, the more it was meant to be).

But when we look back at the embers of failed relationships, what often emerges is that we simply weren't clear enough, with ourselves or with the other, as to what we needed. We failed to see that we had certain implicit requirements that we omitted to explore with necessary forthrightness.

Compare this with our approach at work. It would be odd, when tasked with hiring someone, to conclude that we had to let time take its course. We understand the urgency. No less intense time pressure exists, in a more concealed form, in love (we need only ask an older person about the windows that lie between 20 and 30, and 30 and 40).

When recruiting at work, we also have little compunction about clarity for what a role entails. We understand that there are criteria and that it helps to list them. Somewhere inside, we have comparably defined requirements in love – we're just a lot more hesitant about drawing them up. We might (let's imagine) need someone who is:

interested in psychology

working on themselves

ready to put a relationship above their friends

---

settled in their career

---

neither having nor wanting children

---

keen to travel

---

attractive to us – which probably means not too tall and maybe
with glasses

But to draw out such criteria, we need to understand ourselves – and
then feel sufficiently legitimate and confident about our wishes to dare
to go out into the world in search of them.

We should import into our hunt for love some of the
unembarrassed state of mind that naturally accompanies us in the
workplace. Why wouldn't we use technological tools? Why wouldn't we
set aside a few hours regularly for the search? Why wouldn't we tap our
networks in undisguised ways? Why wouldn't we, on dates, run through
a prescribed set of questions (subtly delivered)? To do anything less
disregards the fundamental basis of our lives: that we have limited time.

Jane Austen would have understood. Every date is, at heart, a
recruitment interview, for which we need to show up with a privately
held brief and the right set of questions. The breadsticks and olives
shouldn't distract us: this is possibly the most serious work of our lives,
given the contribution that love can make to life's richness.

The best way to guarantee our finer, higher emotions may be to
double down on their practical underpinnings: the best guarantor of
love is a very unromantic mindset.

Instructions for creating a job spec for love

1. Set aside dedicated time to reflect deeply on your core requirements in a partner, treating this task with the same seriousness you would give to drafting a professional job description.

2. Write down your non-negotiable criteria first. Be as specific and honest with yourself as you would be when listing essential qualifications for a work position.

3. Consider both personal qualities (emotional intelligence, communication style) and practical factors (lifestyle preferences, future goals) that matter to you.

4. Review past relationships objectively, like analysing previous hiring decisions, to identify patterns in what has and hasn't worked for you.

5. Create a clear timeline for your search, acknowledging that finding love, like professional recruitment, benefits from having structured goals and deadlines.

6. Develop a strategy for where and how you'll conduct your search, including both traditional and digital approaches.

7. Prepare thoughtful questions for your 'interviews' (dates) that will help reveal compatibility with your requirements.

8. Remember to stay open to exceptional candidates who might not perfectly match your spec but could bring unexpected value to your life.

9. Regularly review and update your criteria based on new experiences and insights, just as job specifications evolve with changing needs.

10. Share your requirements with trusted friends who can act as your 'recruitment network' and introduce potential matches.

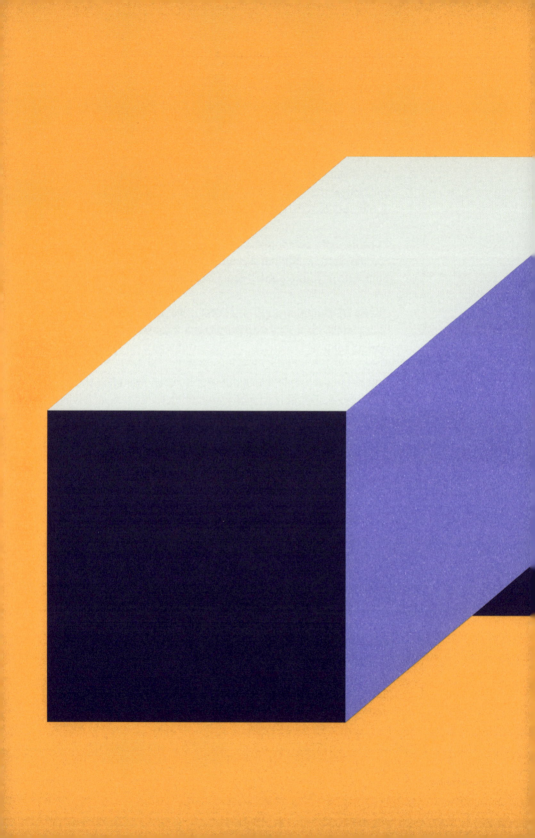

THE SELF

30.
The House-Tree-Person Test

From the moment a child can hold a crayon, their scribbles start to form the universal symbols of their world: the square with a triangle roof for a house, a simple brown trunk with a green blob for a tree and stick figures to represent people.

Drawing on the natural inclination of children to express themselves through art, the psychologist John N. Buck devised the House-Tree-Person test.

1. Find a pen or pencil and a blank sheet of paper.

2. Draw a house.

3. Now, draw a tree next to the house.

4. Finally, draw a person next to the tree and the house.

House drawing

Houses are taken to represent our personal and family lives. Consider the elements you have included and those you have excluded in your house drawing.

Take a look at the doors and windows. Is there a sense of openness or are they more closed off? This may give you an idea of how you approach social connections and barriers.

Look at the walls. How strong or fragile are they? What could this say about your sense of vulnerability?

Have you depicted a chimney? The presence and amount of smoke from a chimney can be symbolic. What does yours say about the level of warmth, spirit or tension in your home? The absence of a chimney might simply reflect that your own home lacked a fireplace, so it didn't cross your mind to draw one. But, symbolically, it could also suggest a deeper story – a sense of distance or coldness tied to the idea of 'home'.

Tree drawing

Tree drawings are said to reflect long-standing, unconscious feelings towards oneself, and particularly the degree to which one is open to support from others.

Observe your tree's overall size and posture. Does it stand tall and proud, or is it more downcast? This can mirror feelings of strength, growth or being overshadowed.

Scars, knotholes or broken branches can indicate past traumas or significant events. What story does your tree tell?

Person drawing

Person drawings are a manifestation of our view of ourselves and who we wish to become.

Consider how you portrayed the arms. Are they open or folded? This may indicate how you tend to engage socially.

Consider the size and direction of the head and the emotions depicted in the person's expression. This could reveal something about how you perceive your own intellect and emotions.

Buck designed the House-Tree-Person test as a projective psychological assessment based on the belief that, through our simple drawings, much can be revealed about our unconscious attitudes and desires.

31.

A Map of Values

What we decide to be our most significant memories are a powerful guide to our core values – which it can otherwise be hard to get close to. With this exercise, you can explore your defining moments to better understand what really matters to you.

1. Think back to a truly meaningful experience in your life. What made it so special for you? Take a pen and paper and describe the experience in writing, as vividly as possible. Capture where you were, the sensations you felt, those who were present and what emotions were there for you. Allow yourself to relive the experience as fully as you can and linger on the details that made it so memorable for you.

2. Once you have written out the story, read it slowly and thoughtfully. With a fine-tooth comb, pick up on the personal values that stand out. For example, you may spot in your story the value of 'sharing a deep connection with others', 'showing bravery', 'being of service' or 'losing yourself in nature'. Highlight and make a list of these values as you notice them. If you're finding it tricky to identify these, you can make use of the list of values on the next page.

3. After identifying these values, create a 'map' of your values, with each in its own bubble. Explore how they might connect or branch into related ideas. For instance, 'adventure' could branch into 'spontaneity', 'openness' and 'bravery'.

**Possible
Values**

accomplishment	friendship	perseverance
accountability	fun	pleasure
adventure	generosity	popularity
ambition	gratitude	power
authenticity	growth	purpose
balance	happiness	recognition
beauty	honesty	reputation
boldness	humility	resourcefulness
challenge	humour	respect
collaboration	influence	responsibility
community	innovation	security
compassion	integrity	self-awareness
competency	justice	self-discipline
confidence	kindness	self-respect
creativity	knowledge	serenity
curiosity	leadership	service
determination	learning	stability
empathy	love	status
equality	loyalty	success
faith	meaningful work	trust
fame	openness	wealth
forgiveness	optimism	wisdom
freedom	peace	

The waypoints for our future can be found in these value maps – a reminder of who we are at our best and what truly makes us feel alive.

As you finish the exercise, take some time to consider your findings. To what extent are your values being honoured? Are there areas in which they feel neglected? Use this as a stopping point to revisit and incorporate your guiding principles more consciously into your life.

Complete the following sentences to expand your reflection:

A value I see clearly enacted in my life is ... because ...

A value I would like to nurture more is ... because ...

One way I can bring more ... into my life is by ...

This exercise has reminded me that ... is truly important to me.

This exercise can be a quiet promise to yourself – a way of remembering what matters most and ensuring your mission is clear as you move forward.

32.

A Self-actualisation Test

One of the most renowned ideas in the history of psychology is located in an unassuming triangle divided into five sections, referred to universally simply as Maslow's 'hierarchy of needs'. This influential pyramid was first presented in 1943, and it has since become a central component of psychological analyses, business presentations and online lectures – and it has grown ever more emphatic in the process.

The pyramid was the work of American psychologist Abraham Maslow, who had been looking, since the start of his professional career, for nothing less than the meaning of life. Maslow wanted to find out what could make life purposeful for people (himself included) in modern-day America – a country where the pursuit of money and fame seemed to have eclipsed more authentic aspirations. He saw psychology as the discipline that would enable him to answer the yearnings and questions that people had once taken to religion.

Maslow proposed that human beings have essentially five different kinds of needs, split between the psychological and the material.

For Maslow, we all start with a set of utterly non-negotiable and basic physiological needs: food, water, warmth and rest. In addition, we have urgent safety needs for bodily security and protection from attack. But then we start to enter the psychological domain. We need a sense of belonging and love; friends and lovers. We need esteem and respect. And lastly, and most grandly, we are driven by what Maslow called an urge for 'self-actualisation': a concept he described as 'living according to one's full potential' and 'becoming who we really are'.

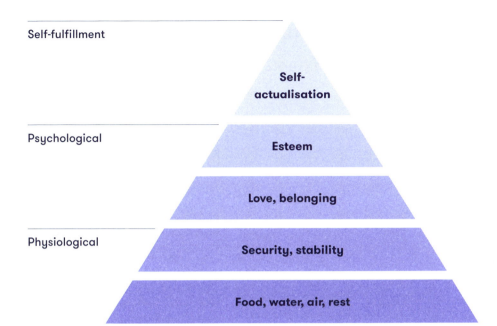

Self-fulfillment

Psychological

Physiological

Self-actualisation

Esteem

Love, belonging

Security, stability

Food, water, air, rest

Maslow was pointing us to the need for a greater balance between the many priorities we must juggle. His beautifully simple visual cue is, above anything else, a portrait of a life lived in harmony with the complexities of our nature. We should, in our less frantic moments, use it to reflect with renewed focus on what it is we might do next.

The following self-actualisation test helps to illuminate that very question, steering us in the direction of the fullest, most authentic expression of ourselves.

Reflect thoughtfully on each statement and indicate the degree to which it aligns with your personal experience:

1 = strongly disagree

2 = disagree

3 = neither agree nor disagree

4 = agree

5 = strongly agree

1. I cherish solitude and find comfort in being alone.

....

2. I rely on my own experiences and judgements to form my opinions.

....

3. I frequently experience moments of ecstasy, harmony and deep meaning.

....

4. I can laugh at myself and do not take myself too seriously.

....

5. I often remind myself of life's simple pleasures.

....

6. I feel a deep sense of care and commitment towards others and my community.

....

7. I am highly attuned to insincerity and disingenuousness in others.

....

8. I often feel an abiding connection and unity with humanity.

....

9. I experience profound compassion for the struggles of others.

....

10. I can deal humourously with the contradictions of the human condition.

....

11. I am motivated by a focus on goals or causes greater than myself.

....

12. I am tolerant and accepting of others' shortcomings.

....

13. I remain authentic to myself, even when faced with external pressures to conform. ....

14. I seek to cultivate deep and meaningful connections with others. ....

15. I prefer having a few close friends to many perfunctory relationships. ....

16. I do not depend heavily on external validation or the approval of others. ....

17. While I value strong relationships, I equally enjoy spending time in my own company. ....

18. I would describe myself as self-sufficient and resourceful. ....

19. I tend not to be swayed by societal norms or external influences in forming my own views. ....

20. I believe I can assess situations with honesty and sound judgement. ....

21. My actions often feel genuine, natural and uncontrived. ....

22. My relationships are marked by deep, loving bonds. ....

23. I can intensely appreciate the beauty of a sunset or a flower, time after time. ....

24. I feel a strong responsibility to contribute meaningfully to society. ....

25. I am dedicated to a personal mission or purpose that drives me. ....

26. I am tolerant of myself, including my flaws and imperfections. ....

27. I feel a sense of unity and affinity with everything around me. ....

Total score:

....

Scoring your answers

Calculate your total score by adding up your responses to each question. Use this score to evaluate where you stand in the direction of self-actualisation.

27–60 points

It may be a struggle for you to live in your own company and to accept imperfections in yourself or others. We have all been there. Areas for growth could include finding a level of comfort in solitude and learning to appreciate simple joys. A stronger sense of your personal mission or purpose could almost certainly support closer alignment with self-actualising qualities.

61–90 points

You may value meaningful relationships and autonomy, but there could be opportunities to nurture, for instance, a deeper sense of community. A focus on learning to accept others' flaws and finding meaning in both solitude and helping others may help this journey.

91–120 points

You demonstrate many of the characteristics of a self-actualised person. These likely include authenticity, a strong sense of compassion and a knack for building strong relationships. Your approach to life is likely marked by spontaneity, a natural alignment with your values and a commitment to a mission or purpose that extends beyond yourself.

121–135 points

You strongly resonate with the principles of self-actualisation and embody them in everyday life. You likely find comfort and joy in being alone, as well as maintaining deep, loving relationships, and you have a persistent freshness in appreciating the simple things in life. It is your sense of purpose, your compassion for others and your ability to deal with obstacles with humour and tolerance that distinguish your outlook.

33. The Premeditation Test

The Stoic philosophers of Ancient Greece and Rome invented the term 'premeditation' to describe a process – normally to be performed once a day in the morning – whereby one looks into one's future and systematically imagines everything that could go wrong. It is a deliberate, artful, ritualised meditation on possible upcoming disasters.

The practice is based on the view that our minds do us an enormous disservice through their sentimental, unexamined optimism, leaving us unprepared for the catastrophes that will inevitably come our way. A premeditation constitutes a deliberate attempt to bring our expectations in line with the troubles we might face.

The Roman philosopher Seneca – possibly the greatest of all the Stoics – believed that the greatest service we can pay ourselves is to anticipate disaster. Here is one of Seneca's premeditations as an example:

> The wise will start each day with the thought: fortune gives us nothing which we can really own. Whatever has been built up over years is scattered and dispersed in a single day. No, he who has said 'a day' has granted too long; an hour, an instant, suffices for the overthrow of empires. Look at your wrists, a falling tile could cut them. Look at your feet, a paving stone could render you unable to walk again. We live in the middle of things which have all been destined to be damaged and to die. Mortal have you been born, to mortals have you given birth. Reckon on everything, expect everything.

Complete each premeditation:

What are you hoping for?

....

....

Premeditate that it won't happen.

Who do you rely on?

....

....

Premeditate that they will let you down.

Who do you love?

....

....

Premeditate that they will leave you.

What are you proudest of?

....

....

Premeditate that it will be ruined.

Consider your reputation.

....

....

Premeditate on its destruction.

Do you expect to live long?

....

....

Premeditate on your possible death before tonight.

Does the ground seem solid?

....

....

Premeditate on an earthquake.

A lot of agitation boils down to a single fear:

If X happens ...	*... I won't be able to survive.*
(Part A)	(Part B)

Notice that there are two parts to that statement: A and B. Most of the time, when people are trying to calm us down, they focus on addressing part A. They spend their time telling us that what we fear will happen, won't happen. This is meant very kindly, and it works in the short term, but it doesn't properly help and, in the long run, does us a serious disservice.

We recommend a different route, concerning part B: to look squarely at what you think you won't survive and realise that, in one way or another, you will. It might be pretty tough, and 'surviving' might be a long way from thriving, but you will get through it one way or another. Increasing our own sense of resilience is vital to calming ourselves down.

It is possible to work on our confidence in our ability to survive. We are, in fact, far stronger and more resilient than we think; a lot of what we have right now, we could lose and do without. We may believe that we'd be broken by various sorts of frustrations and losses, but we could withstand them. We could lose our health, our partner, our job or our status, and it would be unpleasant but survivable.

The way to convince ourselves of this is to think through in detail how life would be possible in a reduced state. We mustn't leave our fears at the back of our minds, unexamined and toxic. We need to bring them out into broad daylight and submit them to reason. We need to envisage a survivable reduced existence.

Prepare answers for the following disasters:

being fired

being disgraced

being abandoned

falling seriously ill

falling into poverty

Seneca was initiating an important move. By continually renewing our acquaintance with our own resilience we can be braver, because we grasp that the dangers we face are almost never as great as our skittish imaginations tend to suggest.

Premeditation doesn't, of course, remove the bad things. But by getting us to admit, frankly and bravely, that we are likely to encounter setbacks in our lives, it can leave us a little less distraught when they eventually come our way.

34. A Self-love Test

One way to start assessing how badly we have been knocked by our early years – and where we might, therefore, need to direct most of our repair work and attention – is to identify a range of markers of emotional health and imagine how we fare in relation to them. Among these, self-love has vital importance, determining how much we can be friends with ourselves and, day to day, remain on our own side.

Consider your answers to these questions:

1. When you meet a stranger who has things you don't, how quickly do you feel pitiful – and how long can you remain assured by the decency of what you have and are?

2. When another person frustrates or humiliates you, can you let the insult go, able to perceive the senseless malice beneath the attack, or are you left brooding and devastated, implicitly identifying with the verdict of your enemies?

3. How much can the disapproval or neglect of public opinion be offset by the memory of the steady attention of a few significant people in the past?

4. In relationships, do you have enough self-love to leave an abusive union? Or are you so down on yourself that you carry an implicit belief that harm is all you deserve?

5. In a different vein, how good are you at apologising to a lover for things that may be your fault?

6. How rigidly self-righteous do you need to be? Can you dare to admit mistakes, or does an admission of guilt or error bring you too close to a background sense of nullity?

7. In the bedroom, how clean and natural or alternatively disgusting and sinful do your desires feel? Might they be a little odd, but not bad or dark, since they emanate from within you and you are not a wretch?

8. At work, do you have a reasonable, well-grounded sense of your worth – and so feel able to ask for (and properly expect to get) the rewards you are due?

9. Can you resist the need to please others indiscriminately?

10. Are you sufficiently aware of your genuine ability to say no?

It isn't our fault – or, in a sense, anyone else's – that many of these questions are so hard to answer in the affirmative. But by entertaining them, we are at least starting to understand what kind of shape our wounds have and, consequently, what kind of bandages might be most necessary.

35. A Self-hatred Audit

One of the odder features of self-hatred is that the affliction may escape our notice for the greater part of our lives. We may simply not be aware that we don't like ourselves very much – even as the sickness of self-hatred wreaks its havoc across a range of psychological situations and opportunities.

Though we are relentless scrutinisers of others, we seldom pause to give a unitary verdict on what we make of our own characters. We may recognise our approval or distaste of ourselves in relation to specific actions; we will know when we are, for example, cross about being slow to complete a task or when we are pleased to have won a colleague's approval. But we are rarely inclined to step far back and consider ourselves as a whole, as we might a stranger. We are too involved with ourselves on an ongoing basis to assess the sharper outlines of our own characters. There are few occasions when we are summoned to ask whether we essentially like the person we are.

As a result, our self-hatred tends to linger in undiagnosed forms. We miss the extent to which we can suffer from endemic self-loathing – and how a once acceptable and perhaps invigorating form of self-questioning has turned into a lacerating sequence of attacks on everything we are and do. We may, paradoxically, be at once highly depressed about ourselves and oblivious that we are so.

In order to know what we are up against, we should take a measure of our sense of self. We can ask to what extent we might agree with the following sentences on a scale of 1–10, with 10 meaning very much and 1 indicating not at all:

1. If people knew who I really am, they would be horrified.

2. The inside of me is appalling.

3. Often, I can't bear who I am.

4. I'm disgusting.

5. I'm shameful.

_____

6. I'm weak.

_____

7. Others have good cause to hate and harm me.

_____

8. It's only a matter of time before terrible things happen to me, given who I am.

_____

9. I'm sexually revolting.

_____

10. I am physically repulsive.

_____

11. I am unworthy of being forgiven.

_____

12. I am a fitting target for ridicule.

_____

13. I am bound to fail.

_____

14. I don't deserve much sympathy.

_____

15. People often see me in the street and feel contempt.

_____

16. I have acted badly across my whole life.

_____

17. There is something fundamentally wrong with me.

_____

We don't need to do careful sums to arrive at an indicative picture at speed. Some of us will be reaching for tens on pretty much every occasion; others – blessedly – will fall into the lower figures.

If we find ourselves reaching for high numbers, we might be tempted to come to a powerful yet entirely mistaken conclusion: that we are terrible people. The reality is less personally damning and far more redemptive. We are not so terrible at all; we are just very ill. The questionnaire is revealing an affliction, not our past or what we deserve or who we really are. The extremity of our answers should signal that something is afoot that far exceeds what any human is ever owed. We aren't intolerably wicked; we are in the grip of a cruel sickness that systematically destroys any confidence or generosity we might feel towards ourselves. We are treating ourselves with a violence and pitilessness we wouldn't bestow upon our worst enemies.

Somehow, unbeknownst to us, we have ended up considering the person we have to accompany through life with an unparalleled degree of coldness and disdain.

It is time to come to terms with our suffering and to refuse the delusion and meanness of self-hatred.

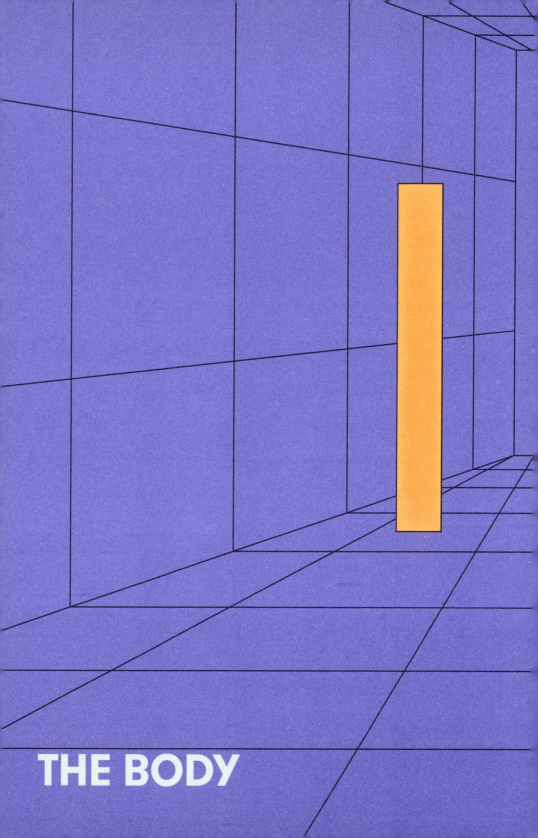

THE BODY

36. What Your Body Reveals about Your Past

For well-founded reasons, we can end up imagining that the main clues to understanding who we are lie in our brains. It must be words and memories that have the best chance of explaining who we really are and what has happened to us.

But this is to ignore the evidence stored in our bodies. As the saying goes, our bodies keep the score. But what is the score, and how can we discover it?

To generalise, our bodies are repositories of pain. The more difficult our trajectory through life has been, the more we are likely to feel negatively towards our bodies and the more troubles they may give us.

Two problems in particular stand out. First, low bodily self-esteem. If our early caregivers did not take delight in our physical form, we may struggle to appreciate our own appearance. We might interpret the gaze of others as hostile, flinch when we catch sight of ourselves in the mirror and feel sorry for our partner, who has the misfortune of having to see us close up. Equally, if a caregiver directed contempt towards our characters, a little of their disdain tends to wash over into our physical self-image. Bad people must – we imagine – also be bad-looking people; we're likely to identify with beetles, earthworms or crows.

A second area in which our bodies function like recording machines is in fear: how on edge or primed for danger do they feel? They may remain permanently vigilant, as though waiting for a blow or attack. We may have trouble sleeping (especially next to another person) and our digestive systems may be unable to unclench – indicators of a past filled with cruel or unpredictable dynamics.

Trauma may also manifest physically. We may find it excruciatingly hard to let our limbs move in an energetic or uninhibited manner. Without being lazy in our lives in general, we might find it very difficult to exercise – simply because this requires us to lose rational command. Dancing might be similarly difficult. Our gait and posture may indicate an ongoing lack of bend and sway.

Despite such hints, we typically overlook what our bodies may be telling us. We assume that they are blank objects without a story to share, and we interpret their baseline state as 'normal'. It is hard to notice that anything might be amiss if we have always felt tense, rigid, or have always hated our appearance. We tend to notice only changes. Our bodies both record the score and assiduously 'forget' it.

Fortunately, we can reverse this amnesiac attitude and 'interview' our bodies with a view to recovering explicit clues about the past.

Questions that pick up on exposure to criticism and contempt:

How much do I like my body?

How much can I expect that someone I like might approve of me physically?

How comfortable do I feel going outside the house?

How does my body feel in public?

What sort of animal might I compare myself to?

How do I feel when I see myself in the mirror?

Do I avoid looking at my reflection or photos of myself?

How often do I assume that others are judging my appearance negatively?

Do I feel deserving of physical affection or admiration?

How do I react to compliments about my appearance?

What memories do I have of others having commented on my physical appearance?

How well do I ordinarily sleep?

What is my digestion like?

How easy or hard is it for me to relax physically?

Are my limbs rigid or loose?

How does my body respond to loud noises or sudden movements?

Do I ever find myself clenching my jaw, fists, or other parts of my body without realising?

How does my body feel when I am dancing?

Just asking the questions can produce intriguing physical effects. The body may feel heard. It might even spasm or vibrate a little as we consider it in a new, compassionate way.

We might want to close our eyes and reassure our bodies that any danger is past, that it is time to unclench ourselves from fear and that we are finally free to share our difficulties.

37.

A Body Language Test

We 'speak' many of our thoughts, feelings and intentions through our bodies, usually with little conscious awareness. Our posture, hand gestures, even subtle twitching of our eyebrows and the angle of our gaze, inadvertently reveal our states of confidence, fear, attraction or unease.

Finish the sentences on the opposite page, focusing exclusively on what you notice regarding your body language across a set of contexts.

At social events

At social events, I find that my posture is …

....

....

When I talk with friends, I often … with my hands.

....

....

....

When listening intently, I …

....

....

When I feel relaxed and comfortable, my facial expressions usually …

....

....

....

If I feel nervous in a social setting, I …

....

....

....

In romantic interactions

When meeting someone I like on a date, my physical demeanour is …

....

....

When I want to show interest, I …

....

....

In intimate conversations, I tend to … with my eyes.

....

....

....

If I feel attracted to a person, I usually …

....

....

....

When I want to show my partner affection, I usually …

....

....

....

In stressful or challenging situations

....

When I'm frustrated or impatient,
I've seen myself ...

....

....

....

When trying to avoid a situation
or topic, I ...

....

....

....

If I'm confronted or challenged,
I tend to ... with my eyes.

....

....

....

Under pressure, I notice that
my breathing ...

....

....

....

When I feel stressed, my shoulders ...

....

....

....

Looking over your answers, what is the broad overall picture? Given that many of our bodily behaviours may be unconsciously driven, we may want to ask a kind and honest friend to give us their impressions and feedback too.

Ideally, we should strive not to allow our anxiety-ridden, overpowering or distracting bodily habits to interfere with how we intend to communicate. With a better grasp of how we hold ourselves nonverbally across different contexts, we can aim for a greater alignment between who we are and what we want our bodies to help us say.

38. | The Hand Test

Our hands are hugely eloquent parts of our bodies. We can hardly get to know someone well without, at some stage, asking to have a close look at their hands.

The Hand Test, invented by psychologist Edwin E. Wagner in the 1960s and later refined by Barry Bricklin and Zygmunt A. Piotrowski, picks up on this intuitive sense. It is a playful exercise founded on the implicit relationship between our hands and our psyches. Presenting us with images of hands engaged in various ambiguous actions, the test requires us to project our own narratives, inferring the action or intended action of each hand and thereby revealing something of our own inner natures.

Look at the following images one at a time and write down what you think the pictured hand might be doing and what its owner might be feeling.

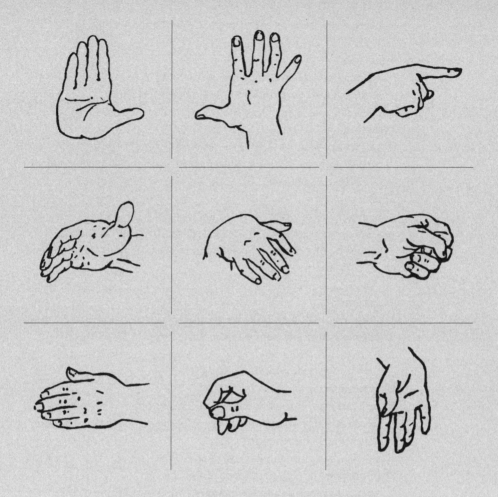

Then, more acutely,
imagine a hand yourself.
Picture what it might
be doing and then try to
draw it (don't worry if
it doesn't look very good).

Here are some interpretations of what your drawing might mean:

Aggression
If you imagined a hand attacking, dominating or forcefully seizing, it suggests comfort with the idea of taking decisive action.

Direction
If you saw the hand as leading or influencing others – pointing out a direction, perhaps – this may reflect an assuredness in guiding people.

Fear:
If the hand was depicted as curled up, it points to heightened awareness of the potential harm caused by others, and a fear of vulnerability and retaliation. What might you be trying to defend yourself from – and why?

Affection
If you envisioned 'shaking hands', 'offering a flower' or 'petting a dog', it suggests a kind and benevolent attitude towards the world and an ease around connection.

Communication
If the hand was pictured as trying to communicate – 'gesticulating in conversation', perhaps – this may reflect a desire to be understood, validated and comprehended.

Dependence
If the hand was seen as seeking another hand to hold, it may point to an ease with reliance on others – but also a degree of fear around independence.

These interpretations are only ever suggestions – not science. Ultimately, you are the best guide to the meaning of your hand drawing (and your hands). What is key – as ever in these tests – is that we are being prompted and encouraged in intriguing ways to reflect on the most important question of all: Who might I really be?

39. Interviewing the Body

An unexpected and troublesome feature of being human is that we feel so much more than we realise we feel. There are emotions coursing through us – of anger or joy, resentment or fear – that lie just outside the sphere of ordinary consciousness, and that elude us as we rush through the challenges of our lives.

And yet, unless the full panoply of our emotions is regularly identified and adequately 'felt', we are likely to fall prey to a range of psychological ills: anxiety, paranoia, depression and worse. Mental unwellness is born out of an accumulation of unfelt feelings.

We must do ourselves the favour of regularly – ideally once a day – carving out periods in which we can get more deeply acquainted with our true emotions. We must continually ask ourselves a simple-sounding but grand and deep question: What am I feeling now?

To draw out valuable answers, we should sit somewhere quiet, probably in bed, with the lights low and a journal and pen handy. We should close our eyes and let the generosity and free-form nature of the question resonate. After a few moments of scanning the penumbra of the inner mind, we are liable to pick up a few intimations of something. It might be the rustle of a disturbingly well-camouflaged anxiety. With some of the stealth of a hunter in the undergrowth or a fisherman by the bank of a river, we can press ourselves to reflect further: What does it seem we are actually anxious about?

It may require a good deal more reverie and inner enquiry before we very gradually begin to feel a recognisable notion emerging, like a landscape subtly appearing at the slow break of a summer day. We may need to decode apparently minute moments of aggression, meanness, confusion or grief that have impacted us without us properly noticing. Or we might, as we examine ourselves, detect traces of ancient traumas that seem to be still active in distant valleys: someone is crying, someone is very worried, a small person – who might be us – needs our help quite badly.

We should carry out a similar process with our bodies, where many more muted feelings lie buried. What is my body feeling?

We can ask, strangely but usefully. What would it like to talk to me about? And to get more specific: If my shoulders could speak right now, what might they say? And my chest, what would it say? And my arms, my hands, my legs, my feet?

Our limbs might want to curl into a ball and long for reassurance, or else hit an opponent, or elongate themselves defiantly and boldly. Or they might remember an old, frustrated wish to be held on a comforting chest.

Use the following questions to reflect on each part of your body to explore the physical and emotional sensations you may be holding:

Eyes
What are my eyes tired of seeing? If they could speak, what would they say they would like to see more and less of?

Ears
What sounds are affecting my ears? What would they want to block out or hear more of?

Neck
If my neck could speak, how would it describe the tension and weight it is carrying?

Shoulders
What burdens do my shoulders feel? What are they holding on to?

Chest
What emotions are sitting in my chest? What would my heart say if it could express itself?

Stomach
What does my stomach feel consumed by? What emotions has it had enough of ingesting?

Back
What kind of support is my back asking for? Who does it feel it can and cannot lean on?

Arms
What would my arms like to let go of or reach out for?

Hands
If my hands could speak, what would they say about the way they have been used? What are they longing to hold, feel or create?

Hips
What emotions feel locked in my hips? How would my hips like to move?

Legs
What are my legs feeling? Are they restless or steady?

Feet
What do my feet long to walk on, stand on, dance on or step away from?

Take the time to listen – your body is always speaking.

40. The Bodily Self-image Test

We carry around with us hugely complicated feelings about our bodies, and especially about different parts of them. Here is a test to help you understand your body better:

1. **With a pen and paper, draw a rough outline of your body.**

2. **Label areas according to how you feel about them:**

    Which parts of yourself make you feel ashamed?

    Which parts of your body do you avoid looking at or thinking about?

    Which areas of your body do you feel proud of or confident about?

    Which parts remind you of someone you love?

    Which parts remind you of someone you don't like?

    Which parts feel like they betray you?

    Which parts of your body feel foreign, like they don't belong to you?

    Which parts of your body do you punish, intentionally or not?

    Which parts of your body do you feel closest to – which do you feel are most 'you'?

3. **With each of your answers, think back to where these particular feelings might have stemmed from. What is the history of your feelings towards your body?**

Where this reflection brings up negative feelings, we can hope – with time – to try to alter the unhelpful verdicts and associations that cling to us. We can, with self-compassion, redraw the emotional maps of our bodies.

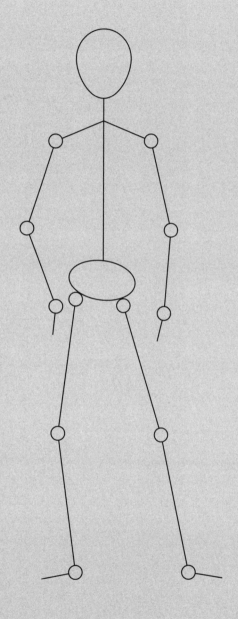

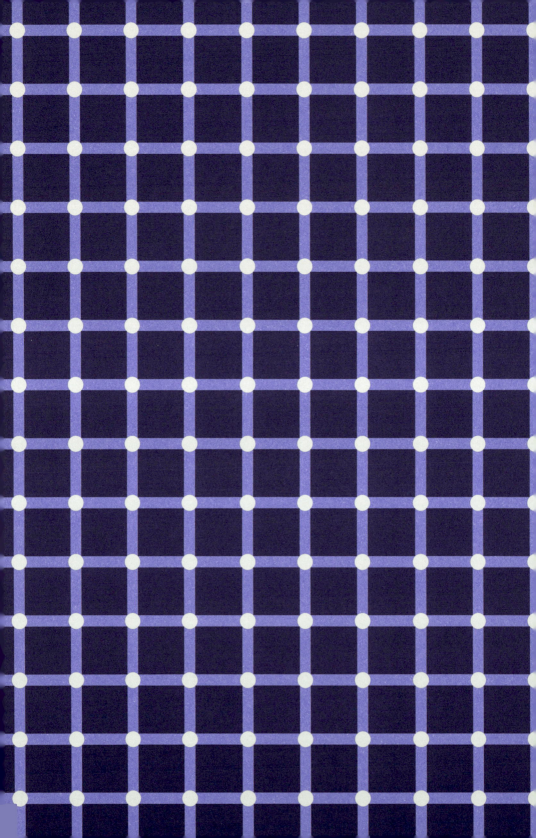

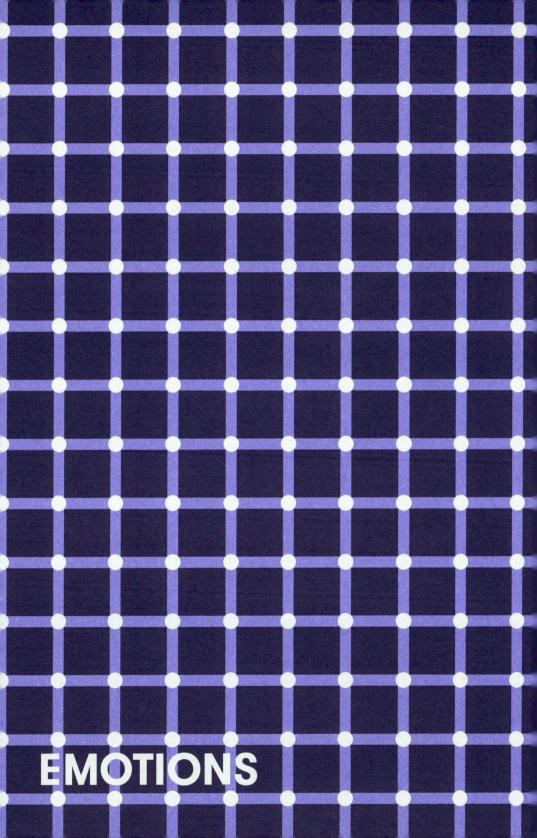

EMOTIONS

41.

A Philosophical Meditation

Our minds are some of the busiest places in the known universe. It is estimated that, under a deceptively calm exterior, some 70,000 separate thoughts hurry through consciousness from the moment we wake up to the time we slip into sleep – some of these elaborate and sequential, many more fragmentary and sensory by nature.

What these many thoughts have in common is that we seldom do them any kind of justice. The river of ideas and feelings is relentless, turbulent and chaotic. In a typical minute, we might briefly register that we are annoyed with a friend, then our minds are directed to a worry about a tax return, which is quickly supplanted by the sighting of a raven, which makes us think of our grandmother, who evokes a trip we once took to Greece, which ushers in thoughts of some lip balm we need to purchase, which is then supplanted by a pain in our left knee, which is succeeded by a memory of a friend we lost touch with after university, which cedes to a recurring reflection on what kind of lamp we might invest in for the living room. And we might here still only be at the thirty-second mark of what we casually call 'thinking' or just 'gazing out of the window'.

The result of this sensory overload is an immense difficulty in processing what we actually experience. We don't have time to feel the anger we are beset by; we don't have the wherewithal to give room to the sadness that nags at us. We can't unpick the promising project that enlivens our ideas of the future. We can't – on so many occasions – properly think our own thoughts or feel our own feelings. Instead, our mental material is cast into the shadows of the unconscious. It is within us but outside of our awareness. We are exiled from our own rage, joy, nostalgia, sympathy and ambition.

This loss is not merely theoretical. We pay a high price for the build-up of unknown experiences inside us. Our feelings and thoughts are in the habit of needing to be understood – and will protest when they are not. We are all equipped with what we might call an emotional conscience that demands that we properly notice what has flowed through us – or else makes us suffer for our ignorance. Anger that hasn't been given its due will emerge as irritability; grief that hasn't been honoured will metastasise into aimlessness and despair; envy that hasn't been unpacked will give birth to bitterness. What we call mental illnesses are usually the outcome of periods of our lives in which we haven't had the strength or opportunity to understand or mourn.

What can appease our troubles is self-exploration. We grow more at peace the more we can finally allow ourselves to know who we are; the more we can feel the lives we actually have.

This underscores the importance of having regular periods of mental processing – occasions when we set out to deliberately rescue from unconsciousness some of the mental material we did not properly fathom when it first manifested itself.

Frustratingly, the required ratio of lived time to processing time is heavily stacked against us. Five minutes of ordinary life might – if we really did it justice – require twenty minutes to unpack. If we wanted to fully 'know' and keep in our sights what had 'happened' in a typical day, we might need to reflect for two weeks. The real story of our lives might necessitate a thousand volumes.

But we shouldn't let these sorts of figures undermine more modest and steady effort. There is still enormous validity in simply carving out a few minutes every day to rescue some of what we have been through. Even knowing we have a responsibility to process is an advance on normal functioning.

Here are five questions that we might all cycle through during a session of examination – five questions carefully picked to direct our minds towards areas we tend to neglect, and from where trouble can most intensely arise when we do so.

1. What am I really worried about?

This question recognises something rather unusual about how we operate: we frequently do not stop to ask ourselves what we are truly worried about. This sounds odd. Surely if we are worried, we would be expected to pause rather quickly and explore why? But our minds seem not to work in this supremely logical-sounding way: they feel anxious long before they are ever motivated to ask themselves why they might be so. They can carry on for months, even years, under the fog of diffuse concern before setting themselves the challenge of zeroing in on what is really at stake. So, this question bids us to stop running and instead turn around to look at what might actually be ailing us.

The use of the word 'really' is strategic. We often use one worry to shield us from another. We worry about an upcoming interview to protect us from worrying about the state of our relationship. We worry about money in order not to worry about death. So it can be helpful to keep a supplementary enquiry in mind: What worry might lie behind the worry that is currently obsessing me?

2. What am I presently sad about?

We can make a generalisation: we go around being far braver than is good for us. Because we need to get on with the practicalities of the day, we frequently push to the side all the slights, hurts, disappointments and griefs that flow through our river of consciousness. We choose not to notice how vulnerable we are for fear that we cannot afford our own sensitivity.

But stoicism and strength carry their own dangers. With the help of this question, we should give time to noticing that – despite our competent and strong exteriors – lots of smaller and larger things managed to hurt us today, like every day: perhaps someone didn't laugh when we told a joke, our partner has been a little distant of late, a friend didn't call, or a senior figure at work was less than completely impressed with us.

We don't need to mock ourselves. We aren't weaklings for being fragile. In fact, there is no clearer evidence of our maturity than our capacity to explore the ways in which we, like everyone else on the planet, are as sensitive and easily bruised as a child.

3. Who has annoyed me and how?

We want to be polite. We're attached to the norms of civilisation. It upsets us to think we might be upset. Nevertheless, here too we must have the courage of our actual sensitivity. Not one day goes by without someone annoying us in a rather fundamental way – usually without them in any way meaning to. Our spirits will be lighter if we can bring ourselves to spell out the injury. What happened? How did it make us feel? What might we tell ourselves to refind equilibrium? If we were lucky, we used to do this with a kindly parent when we returned home from school. Now, as careful guardians to ourselves, we can internalise the process and use our inner adult to soothe the always easily flustered but also easily calmed inner child.

4. What does my body want?

Much of what we feel but don't process has a habit of ending up in our bodies. That's why we develop backache, tense shoulders, knotted stomachs and fluttery hearts. In order to live more easily around our bodies, we should regularly drain them of the emotions that they have unfairly been burdened with. We should mentally scan our bodies from top to toe and ask ourselves what each organ might require. What do my shoulders want to tell me? What would my stomach want to say? What does my back need? What do my legs crave? The questions may sound strange; what is surprising is that we are likely to have some very clear answers just waiting for us when we ask.

5. What is still lovely?

Despite so much that is difficult, every day reveals a range of things that delight and enchant us. Often, these elements are small: the light on the kitchen wall in the morning; a child holding its parent's hand at the bus stop; a fig we had at lunchtime. They might not sound like things we should bother to register, but summoned up in their full richness and held in our attention for a few moments, they can help to fortify us against the voices of despair.

We tend to assume that if something is lovely, it will strike our minds with full force, without us needing to do anything supplementary. The reality is stranger: we need to make a conscious effort to squeeze joy out of beneficial moments that might otherwise be forgotten without notice. Our lives have some lovely aspects to them – but we may, surprisingly, regularly and rather clumsily have to make a list of them in order to realise that they exist.

To ask ourselves these questions can feel artificial, we recognise. Surely, if they were so necessary, nature would have found a way to get us to rehearse them automatically. But that is to miss how much that is crucial requires us to submit ourselves to artificial rules. We won't be healthy in our bodies without tediously walking a certain number of steps every day and consuming a given amount of fruit – and, just as annoyingly, our minds won't be in a good place without forcing ourselves to undertake a set of mental exercises to clear up the backlog of unprocessed experiences.

When Socrates, apparently the wisest man of antiquity, was asked to define our highest purpose as humans, he offered a still-legendary answer: 'To know ourselves.' We should aspire to be people who never cease to try to make sense of themselves at the close of every day. We should devote ourselves to constantly trying to shrink the scale of the darkness within us – bringing what was once in shadow closer to the light of interpretation, so that we stand a chance of being slightly less frantic and rather more joyful, creative and calm.

42. The Giant Tear

Some of the most impactful exercises are the simplest. Sometimes we just need a very basic prompt to get us to do what we were on the edge of doing all along but just required permission for.

What is the emotional pain you are carrying? What hurts right now?

Here is a giant tear: write what you have in mind.

43.

How Emotionally Mature Are You?

However old we might be, none of us are ever quite emotionally mature – but having a list to hand of what maturity consists of might be a way to keep score and nudge ourselves in the right direction. Here is a comprehensive list of what maturity might comprise.

Put a tick next to the statements that apply to you. Give yourself 1 point for each statement you tick. Answer honestly to get the most accurate picture of your emotional maturity.

1. You realise that most of other people's bad behaviour really comes down to fear and anxiety – rather than, as it is generally easier to presume, nastiness or idiocy. You loosen your hold on self-righteousness and stop thinking of the world as populated by either monsters or fools. It makes things less black and white at first, but, in time, a great deal more interesting.

2. You understand that what is in your head can't automatically be understood by other people. You realise that, unfortunately, you will have to articulate your intentions and feelings with the use of words – and you can't fairly blame others for not getting what you mean until you've spoken calmly and clearly.

3. You admit that you do sometimes get things wrong. With huge courage, you take your first faltering steps towards (once in a while) apologising.

4. Your confidence is not based on a conviction that you are great, but on an understanding that everyone else is just as stupid, scared and lost as you are. We're all making it up as we go along, and that's fine.

○ 5. You stop suffering from impostor syndrome because you can accept that there is no such thing as legitimacy. We are all, to varying degrees, attempting to act a role while keeping our follies and wayward sides at bay.

○ 6. You forgive your parents because you realise that they didn't put you on this earth in order to insult you. They were just painfully out of their depth and struggling with demons of their own. Anger turns, at points, to pity and compassion.

○ 7. You appreciate the enormous influence of so-called 'small' things on your mood: bedtimes, blood sugar and alcohol levels, degrees of background stress ... As a result, you learn never to bring up an important, contentious issue with a loved one until everyone is well rested, no one is drunk, you've had some food, nothing else is alarming you and you aren't rushing to catch a train.

○ 8. You recognise that when people close to you nag you, or are unpleasant or vindictive, they usually aren't just trying to wind you up; they may be trying to get your attention in the only way they know how. You learn to detect the desperation beneath your loved one's less impressive moments – and, on a good day, you interpret them with love rather than judging them.

○ 9. You give up sulking. If someone hurts you, you don't store up the hatred and the hurt for days. You remember you'll be dead soon. You don't expect others to know what's wrong. You tell them straight and, if they get it, you forgive them. If they don't, in a different way, you forgive them too.

○ 10. You understand that because life is so very short, it's extremely important that you try to say what you really mean, focus on what you really want, and tell those you care about that they matter immensely to you. Probably every day.

○ 11. You cease to believe in perfection in pretty much every area. There aren't any perfect people, perfect jobs or perfect lives. Instead, you pivot towards an appreciation of what is (to use the psychoanalyst Donald Winnicott's exemplary phrase) 'good enough'. You realise that many things in your life are at once quite frustrating and yet eminently good enough.

How to Understand Yourself

12. You recognise the virtues of being a little more pessimistic about how things will turn out – and, as a result, you emerge as a calmer, more patient and more forgiving soul. You lose some of your idealism and become a far less maddening person (less impatient, less rigid, less angry).

13. You can see that everyone's weaknesses of character are linked to counterbalancing strengths. Rather than isolating their weaknesses, you look at the whole picture: yes, someone is rather pedantic, but they're also beautifully precise and a rock in times of turmoil. Yes, someone is a bit messy, but at the same time they're brilliantly creative and very visionary. You realise that perfect people don't exist – and that every strength will be tagged with a weakness.

14. You practise the virtue of compromise. You learn to settle in certain areas and recognise that you're being mature rather than weak when you do so. You might put up with some inconveniences because you know that a friction-free life is a mirage.

15. You fall in love a bit less easily. When you were less mature, you could develop a crush in an instant. Now, you're poignantly aware that everyone, however externally charming or accomplished, would be a bit of a pain from close up.

16. You appreciate that you are quite a difficult person to live with. You shed some of your earlier sentimentality towards yourself. You go into friendships and relationships offering others kindly warnings of how and when you might prove a challenge.

17. You can forgive yourself for your errors and foolishness. You realise the unfruitful self-absorption involved in flogging yourself for past misdeeds. You become more of a friend to yourself. Of course you're an idiot, but you're still a loveable one, as we all are.

18. You realise that part of what maturity involves is making peace with the stubbornly child-like bits of you that will always remain. You cease trying to be a grown-up on every occasion. You accept that we all have our regressive moments – and when your inner 2-year-old rears their head, you greet them generously and give them the attention they need.

19. You stop putting too much hope in grand plans for the kind of happiness that you expect to last for years. You celebrate the little things that go well. You realise that satisfaction comes in increments of minutes. You're delighted if one day passes without too much bother. You take a greater interest in flowers and the evening sky. You develop a taste for small pleasures.

20. What people in general think of you ceases to be such a concern. You realise that the minds of others are muddled places and you don't try so hard to polish your image in everyone else's eyes. What counts is that you and one or two others appreciate you for being you.

21. You get better at hearing feedback. Rather than assuming that anyone who criticises you is either trying to humiliate you or is making a mistake, you accept that maybe it would be an idea to take a few things on board. You can listen to a criticism and survive it, without having to put on your armour and deny there was ever a problem.

22. You realise the extent to which you tend to live, day by day, in too great a proximity to certain of your problems and issues. You remember – more and more – that you need to get perspective on things that pain you. You take more walks in nature; you might get a pet (they don't fret like we do); you appreciate the distant galaxies above us in the night sky.

23. You cease to be so easily triggered by people's negative behaviour. Before getting furious or riled up or upset, you pause to wonder what they might really have meant. You realise that there may be a disjuncture between what someone said and what you immediately assumed they meant.

24. You recognise how your distinctive past colours your response to events and learn to compensate for the distortions that result. You accept that, because of how your childhood went, you have a predisposition to exaggerate in certain areas. You become suspicious of your own first impulses around particular topics. You realise – sometimes – not to go with your feelings.

○ 25. When you start a friendship, you realise that other people don't principally want to know your good news but rather to gain an insight into what troubles and worries you, so that they can feel less lonely about the pains of their own hearts. You become a better friend because you see that what friendship is really about is sharing vulnerability.

○ 26. You calm your anxieties not by telling yourself that everything will be fine. In many areas, it won't. Instead, you build up a capacity to think that even when things go wrong, they are broadly survivable. You realise that there is always a plan B, that the world is broad, that a few kindly souls are always to be found and that the most horrid things are, in the end, endurable.

Scoring your answers

Add up your total points from 0 to 26 to get a picture of your emotional maturity, and where there is space to improve.

0–8
You may often find yourself caught in the throes of self-righteousness and quick judgement, leaving little room for nuance. Forgiveness can seem an insurmountable task. There is no shame in being here; we are all works in progress. You may still be gathering the strength to mature, and small shifts in perspective can lead to a deeper emotional understanding over time.

9–18
You have started to see life as more than a binary formula. You may be letting go of old beliefs, practising forgiveness (even if you occasionally wobble) and learning to marvel at the messiness of human beings. You might notice the value in a compromise here or there, and catch yourself pausing before reacting to others' mishaps. There is a path ahead of you – sometimes clumsy, sometimes graceful, but deeply worthwhile. You can rejoice in the progress you have made, and be assured that the unfolding is only just beginning.

19–26
You approach life with a calm, quiet confidence. You have an awareness that everyone, including yourself, is a mixture of strengths and frailties – and that is precisely our nature. Forgiveness, for yourself

and others, comes naturally. You know that, in the end, there can never be perfection, and you have grown to treasure the 'good enough'. You delight in life's small pleasures and stay calm when pressure mounts. Keep nurturing these qualities – your potential, as ever, is boundless.

Emotional maturity is an ongoing lesson. We are never done with 'growing up'. We can use this list as a starting point to help identify where we are and where we would like to go.

44. What Is Your Safe Place?

For some of us, a 'safe place' might be associated with the enveloping silence of a library, or we might find solace in a favourite living room chair. Going further back, we might recall the atmosphere of our grandmother's kitchen, with its distinctive clatter of dishes and the smell of simmering pots on the stove.

As we think about the spaces we associate with safety, it is helpful to reflect on what it is that makes these places uniquely welcoming and comforting: is it the softness of the pillows, the familiarity of the surroundings or the presence of cherished people?

The following exercise designed by psychotherapist Cathy Malchiodi helps us to visualise our own safe place as a way to calm and reassure us.

1. Start with a relaxation method. Once relaxed, think of all the places, real and imaginary, that have felt safe during your life.

2. Make a list of all the characteristics of your safe places (for example, things that are comfortable, such as pillows, favourite clothes, furniture; things that are familiar; and things that you enjoy having around).

3. Using pens or pencils, draw one safe place; it may be a simple diagram or an elaborate illustration. Add any features that will enhance the safety of the place or make it more comfortable.

4. Look at the image and describe the significance and purpose of each characteristic or feature you included. Imagine yourself standing in this safe place. What would you see to the left and right of you, in front of you, above and below you?

5. Look at your image and consider under what circumstances your safe place would be most helpful to you.

6. Develop a picture in your mind of your safe place and practise visualising it during difficult moments. What does it feel like to visit this place in your imagination?

The safe place is always there, ready for you when you need it.

The safe places we choose tell us key things about what we need in order to feel at peace. Maybe we are drawn to the comfort of a familiar setting, like our childhood bedroom filled with keepsakes, or perhaps we are drawn to more remote places, like a cabin in the woods or a desert. Maybe we need a lot of order or like things to be unkempt. Some of us may be prone to add boundaries – a locked door, a sturdy gate or a wall – to keep the world at bay. Others place more emphasis on warmth, nestling in blankets, dim lighting and ambient noise.

Whatever their form, all these spaces offer hints as to how, through our pasts, our sense of safety emerged, and where we now need to go in our imaginations to relocate the distinctive calm we deserve.

45. Window-staring Exercise

We tend to reproach ourselves for staring out of the window. We are supposed to be working, studying or ticking things off our to-do list. It can seem almost the definition of wasted time. It seems to produce nothing, to serve no purpose. We equate it with boredom, distraction, futility. The act of cupping your chin in your hands near a pane of glass and letting your eyes drift into the middle distance does not normally enjoy high prestige. We don't go around saying, 'I had a great day: the high point was staring out of the window.' But maybe in a better society, that's just the sort of thing people would say to one another.

The point of staring out of a window is, paradoxically, not to find out what is going on outside. It is, rather, an exercise in discovering the contents of our own minds. If we do it right, staring out the window offers a way for us to listen out for the quieter suggestions and perspectives of our deeper selves.

For this exercise, arrange for a quiet interlude by a window, ideally one with a view onto a street or landscape. From this vantage point, notice what you have, of late, been oblivious to: the slow drift of clouds, the gentle sway of grass and leaves in the breeze, the shifting shadows of people hurrying to or from work. As you do so, pay close attention to what is going on within you. Listen to the quieter parts of yourself and allow thoughts and feelings to surface.

Set a timer to spend fifteen minutes on this exercise. When the timer is up, use the following reflective questions to guide your exploration:

As I began staring out of the window, I noticed …

_____

I started becoming aware of thoughts or feelings within me that were …

_____

As I let go of distractions, I noticed my mind drifting towards …

Plato suggested a metaphor for the mind: our ideas are like birds fluttering around in the aviary of our brains. But in order for the birds to settle, Plato understood that we need periods of purpose-free calm. Staring out the window offers such an opportunity. We see the world going on: a patch of weeds is holding its own against the wind; a grey tower block looms through the drizzle. But we don't need to respond; we have no overarching intentions, and so the more tentative parts of ourselves have a chance to be heard, like the sound of church bells in the city once the traffic has died down at night.

The potential of daydreaming isn't recognised by societies obsessed with productivity. But some of our greatest insights come when we stop trying to be purposeful and instead respect the creative potential of reverie. Window daydreaming is a strategic rebellion against the excessive demands of immediate (but ultimately insignificant) pressures, in favour of the diffuse, but very serious, search for the wisdom of the unexplored deep self.

46.

The Cognitive Distortions Test

When we can accept that our minds are rather unreliable instruments, we are better placed to see the need for other minds that we can lean on in order to recalibrate our perspective and re-attune our levels of fear or panic, doubt or despair.

It was with something of this ambition that, in the US in the late 1960s, two American psychologists, Aaron Beck and Albert Ellis, developed a form of therapy that we know today as cognitive behavioural therapy (CBT) – one of the most influential and compelling of all mainstream therapeutic methods. CBT was designed to help clients suffering from three especially pervasive and stubborn mental complaints generated by trauma: anxiety, depression and obsessive thoughts.

Beck and Ellis insisted that patients tormented by this painful trinity were not to be termed 'ill' in any blanket or indiscriminate way. They were to be thought of as, first and foremost, beset by distinctive varieties of flawed or erroneous *thinking* – what Beck and Ellis termed 'cognitive distortions' – and that if only these twisted patterns of thoughts could be identified and pointed out to clients in therapy and then made into objects of study, they might loosen their hold on sufferers' minds and herald a significant shift in mood. The anxious, depressed or obsessive were not 'mad' or inherently damaged, argued Beck and Ellis; they were – once one listened closely to what they were saying – simply in the grip of certain eminently classifiable and alterable errors of reasoning.

In order to facilitate their treatment, Beck and Ellis drew up a list of cognitive distortions that to this day underpins the work of CBT therapists and is typically given to clients at the start of their first session. Among these distortions, we find the following:

1. Catastrophising

The central problem of those dominated by catastrophic thinking is that they have very little idea that they are remotely responsible for thinking in such a way. They remain wholly convinced that they are analysing their particular situation with impeccable and immutable logic, even as they ruthlessly mangle the facts, blur the evidence, jump from one shaky premise to another and concoct conclusions from a medley of fantasies and ogre-filled nightmares. Confident of the solidity of their minds, they have no chance whatsoever to be on guard against their own deductions.

In the circumstances, the first task of the CBT therapist is to make catastrophists aware that they might be such a thing; it is to render them suspicious of their deductive logic in the name of one day helping them to approach their situation with greater solidity and wisdom. Part of healing involves teaching them to become increasingly distrustful of how they are reaching their ideas. Is it really true, a CBT therapist might probe, that one unkind joke means that everyone hates them, or that a single critical voice has to mean the end of every single professional hope? The CBT therapist can concede that not everything might have gone perfectly, but does this have to mean that total and wholesale disaster are also inevitable and imminent? With gentleness and compassion, the sufferer is nudged to perceive how much they might be catapulting themselves into despairing analyses that are scarcely warranted by the evidence on the ground.

2. Favouring emotions over facts

One of CBT's favourite mantras is that 'feelings are not facts' – a way of drawing attention to sufferers' tendencies to insist on interpretations of events that owe little to what has actually happened and everything to the internal voices and presumptions that are being overlaid across reality. It might seem as if an email was saying a particular ominous thing, but was that actually what was said? One might feel as if an ex-partner was unbearably angry, but did they really express any rage? To what extent is one filling in blanks? On what basis is one coming to a particular verdict? Once again, the CBT therapist attempts to prime a sufferer to be more sceptical in the face of their mind's rock-solid and harrowing suppositions.

3. Discounting the positive

As CBT therapists know, what tends to underpin anxiety, depression and obsession are vicious forms of self-hatred. The sufferer expects the worst because they feel themselves to be the worst. Therefore, one of the early tasks of therapy is to keep pointing out how much effort the sufferer is surreptitiously expending on filtering out all positive news about themselves in order to cling with manic fervour to the darkness. If everyone hates us as much as we insist, CBT asks, why then have we been asked out to dinner a number of times of late? If we're a complete failure, how come we enjoy rather a lot of respect at work? If everything is terrible, why does someone nevertheless love us?

4. Mental filtering

CBT therapists will speak of a 'mental filter' that is placed across our minds and doesn't let in any grain of news that might point towards kindness, hope, calm or worthiness. As ever, the task is to alert the sufferer to the existence of such a filter so that its unfairness may become easier to spot and protest against. We aren't necessarily horrific or doomed; what is sure is that there is an extremely unforgiving piece of material covering up the access point between us and the world at large. Apparently, every story in the news is ushering in a given viewpoint, but how representative is our access to news? Who and what are we reading? What have we – in the interests of self-torture – chosen not to listen to?

5. Magnification and minimisation

Two other related terms that CBT wishes to attune us to are 'magnification' and 'minimisation'. As sufferers, we magnify whatever is difficult and worrying, and minimise whatever is kind and good – all without, of course, the slightest awareness that we might be doing so. We continue to insist that our minds can be relied upon, even as they gravely skew and muddle the rich and diverse data that comes their way.

Challenging how we are thinking is at the heart of CBT therapy. A therapist will typically probe at our foremost convictions, laying them out for us to see in a way that we might energetically have avoided doing hitherto. For example: *I have done something very bad for which I can never be forgiven.* Or: *Absolutely no one can be trusted.* Or: *I am cosmically hateful and eternally alone.* And then the therapist might encourage us to ask – with tact and loving scepticism – *but is any of this actually true?*

Unusually, CBT is keen on giving participants homework to complete between sessions. A CBT therapist might ask their client to keep a log of all their most panicky, despairing thoughts – and then every few hours, to submit each one of them to patient reason so as to disarm their customary injustice. Has someone actually harmed us? Have we really offended a friend? What did that person really say? And so on, until the mind slowly learns to disentangle its nets of self-loathing.

Some of the homework can involve deliberately exposing oneself to situations that one has falsely concluded must go a certain way, in order to test one's premises. The person convinced that everyone will hate them might try calling a friend; someone afraid that everyone is mocking them might dare to walk down the street and so observe that everyone is far too wrapped up in themselves to give them a moment's thought.

A conclusion that anyone who submits themselves to CBT should quickly reach is that their mind really doesn't work very well at all. This could sound worrying and sad, but it is in fact the very opposite; it is at the heart of hope and healing, for once we know that our reasoning is in the hands of malevolent, unreliable demons, we can start to set in place some guardrails to protect ourselves against the self-destructive, appalling conclusions that we keep being drawn to. It's by knowing that we can't think too well that we may start to think with a little more fairness and accuracy.

How to Understand Yourself

1. When you notice your mood getting worse, or that you are engaging in unhelpful behaviour or thinking patterns, try to identify which cognitive distortion might be at play. Here is a full list:

Cognitive distortion	Example
All-or-nothing thinking	If I don't pass all my exams with top grades, I'm a failure
Catastrophising	If things don't work out, I'll be so upset, I won't be able to function at all
Disqualifying or discounting the positive	I did get good feedback on the presentation, but that doesn't mean I'm competent
Emotional reasoning	I know I do a lot of things fairly well at work, but I still feel like a failure
Labelling	I'm a loser and a coward
Magnification/ minimisation	Getting a mediocre evaluation proves how inadequate I am; getting high marks doesn't mean I'm smart
Mental filter (selective abstraction)	My boss gave me lots of positive feedback but mentioned one area I could improve on, so I must be doing a terrible job
Mind-reading	My date thinks that I'm boring and not worth the effort
Over-generalisation	Because I felt awkward at the party, I don't have what it takes to make friends
Personalisation	My partner was short with me because I did something wrong
'Should' and 'must' statements	It's terrible that I missed a key point in the brief; I must work harder so I don't make mistakes
Tunnel vision	My colleague can't do anything right – they are lazy, unreliable and terrible at their job

2.   Then ask yourself the following questions:

Can I identify a cognitive distortion?

What's another way to look at this?

If the worst happens, what could I do then?

What's the best that could happen?

What will probably happen?

What could happen if I changed my thinking?

What would a beloved friend want to tell me now?

What would it be good to do now?

The above questions invite us to view our thoughts through a sharper, more discerning lens, recognising them for what they are: interpretations in our minds, rather than unbudgeable realities in the world. As the great mantra of CBT theory puts it: *feelings are not facts.*

47. What Are Your Defence Mechanisms?

Whatever lip service we may pay to the project of self-knowledge, we would, it seems, not like to know much about our identities.

In order to shield us from ourselves, we rely on techniques known as 'defence mechanisms': a range of astonishingly clever internal manoeuvres that subtly enable us to expel uncomfortable ideas from awareness without alerting our conscience, and so return us to a blind, placid equilibrium. It is thanks to defence mechanisms that we're able to convince ourselves that we hate someone we're actually drawn to (but can't have); or that we get depressed in lieu of getting angry with a person who has done us wrong, but who we want to believe is good.

However effective they may be, defence mechanisms ultimately impose a great psychic cost on us; they tie up our energies, repressing ideas on which our growth relies. They mire us in symptoms and secondary illnesses. Every denied thought creates a drag on our minds; every unfelt feeling generates an underground whirlpool of repressed energy. Our defences buy us short-term calm at the expense of long-term development.

Developing an understanding of the way our defence mechanisms work won't magically save us from relying on them, but it may give us an inkling of what our minds are up to, and increase our tolerance to insight.

None of us are without defences. What we call a person's character is in large measure the result of the particular set of defence mechanisms they rely on; it's the outcome of the distinctive ways in which they have opted to defend themselves against the painful sides of their reality.

A list of our defence mechanisms might include the following:

1. | **The grandiose defence**

Once upon a time, we felt catastrophically insignificant. We may have been humiliated and ignored by our caregivers and denied a basic sense that we had a right to exist. As adults, we make use of money, reputation and cultural capital to insist on a specialness that we can't ever truly believe in. We wield grandiosity as a shield against the risks of any renewed encounter with the neglected, powerless and desperate child still sobbing and forlorn somewhere inside us.

2. | **The common-sense defence**

We are filled with huge and painfully complicated truths – they might be about sexuality, love or money. There is so much that we might need to think about and would, as a result, need to mourn or grapple anxiously with. But we lack the courage and wherewithal to do so, and therefore settle on a highly consoling line of defence: that the whole field of psychology is simply 'psychobabble'. We dismiss its efforts as nonsense; we pride ourselves on calling a spade a spade and cling fervently to the solacing thought that our minds lack any of the waywardness, complexity or folly that seem to be the universal lot.

3. | **The manic defence**

We run strenuously from one project to another; we give ourselves no time at all to sit with our odder wishes and fears. It might have been a year since we last had a day without commitments. We devote manic energy to something, anything – work, the news, exercise, literature, drugs, gardening – to keep our unresolved thoughts at bay. The most terrifying prospect in the world might be to simply sit in a silent room with ourselves.

4. | **The sadistic defence**

We choose to feel strong and in control by subjecting another to the pains we once endured as children. We make a junior colleague feel inept; we ensure our offspring knows how little they are worth; we criticise our partner for their countless departures from perfection. There are, in our minds, only two roles a person can play: the victim or the perpetrator. And we have firmly decided the one we'd rather be.

5. The masochistic defence

We feel too weak to prevent ourselves from suffering, but not too weak to turn our suffering into a sort of choice – even, in a manner of speaking, a kind of pleasure. So, we go in search of partners who won't fulfil us, we make sure we criticise ourselves in the wake of every success, we gain a particular relish in being treated badly once again. We know we are going to suffer, but at least – this time around – we are in charge of inflicting the pain on ourselves.

6. The avoidant defence

We might like to be close to others. But because certain people hurt us intolerably when we originally tried to be so, we have come to an easier and more bearable position: we don't, in fact, need anyone at all. We tell ourselves that emotional connection is overrated; we very much enjoy sport or needlework and would – sincerely – far prefer to spend the weekend, or the rest of our lives, in our own company.

7. The early retirement defence

There is much that is – troublingly – rather great about us. We are clever, we can be charming, we might triumph socially or professionally. But such victories carry enormous risks. Someone we once relied on for survival was not comfortable with our success; someone preferred if we messed up. And so we fail repeatedly out of subterranean loyalty to a threatening and threatened caregiver. Internally hemmed in by an invisible choice between victory and abandonment, we retire early from the perils of victory. People wonder why we gave up some pursuit or other. 'They showed so much promise,' they muse, and that – of course – was precisely the problem.

8. The self-hatred defence

Someone was once very unkind to us; someone once left us feeling frightened and insignificant. In all fairness, we should hate them back with equal measure, but that would be too wounding to our innate modesty and we wish to think well of the people in whose care we began. So we rely on an alternative fiction: that our caregivers were fine enough – the problem lay with us. We were not treated abysmally; we just happen to be awful. Harm wasn't done to us; we are entirely stupid or ugly. We deem our problems to be deserved, rather than encountering a greatly more troubling thought: someone we adored was very cruel to us.

9. The magical defence

The laws of science can be abysmally harsh, so we will likely develop a chronic disease within a few years. The laws of economic and romantic probability can be as arduous, so we may never come into great wealth or meet an ideal partner. And precisely because the truth is so vile, we tinker with the basic premises of reality. If we eat the root of a certain plant, if we adopt a particular conspiracy theory, chant a certain mantra or visualise health or success hard enough, we will defeat the 'rational' naysayers. Magical thinking turns despair into delusion.

10. The cynical defence

There can be protection in cynicism, too. We resort to cynicism to avoid the torment of our own expectations. It becomes easier to believe we are doomed, that life is inherently awful and that satisfaction is always a mirage, than to risk the further torments of promise.

Think about which of these mechanisms of defence you notice in yourself and make brief notes about what evidence you are basing your diagnosis on, and in what situation they have occurred.

Weaning ourselves off relying on these defence mechanisms is the work of a lifetime. We don't easily let go of techniques that are so effective at sparing us pain. Surrendering these mechanisms requires a leap of faith – to trust that the price will eventually be worth it, that our symptoms will abate the more we understand them and that we will live more easily once we nurture the roots of self-awareness. Being a true adult – that ever-elusive goal – might mean being someone who no longer needs to deny their real thoughts and feelings; someone willing at last to pay the price for knowing their truth.

How to Understand Yourself

48. Automatic Writing

Usually when we set out to write, our central priorities are to sound coherent and polished. We may think hard before setting anything down; we keep an eye on spelling; we may go back and correct words that don't feel entirely right; we may delete a paragraph or two – all in the hope of eventually reaching a point where what we have articulated seems accurately to reflect what we truly think.

But there is another philosophy of writing that has a very different thesis as to what 'good' writing might be like. While also believing that the ultimate ambition of writing should be the expression of our genuine thoughts, this technique proposes that our best chances of reaching such thoughts lie in making every effort not to think too much, not to agonise about every word, not to go back and correct anything – and instead, just to write down everything that comes into our minds the very moment it does so, without any interest in seeming logical, elegant, clever or even very sane.

This approach, known as automatic writing, asks us to begin by picking an important emotional topic – for example, 'My mother', 'My father', 'My partner' or 'What I really want' – and then writing as fast as we possibly can, for two minutes straight, without a single pause, which can feel like a very exhausting and peculiar requirement indeed.

In a notebook or journal, give yourself two minutes to write down anything that comes to mind on the following topics:

My mother ...

My father ...

My partner ...

What I really want ...

There is still enough time to ...

If I wasn't so scared, I would …

_____

I let myself down when …

When we stand back and read what has tumbled out of us, our feelings about our parents, partners or desires may emerge as very different from what we had presumed. We might find hatred where we had expected love, or love where we had imagined disdain. We might discover layers of longing, envy, rage or sadness that we had kept at bay in our daily lives in the name of appearing that most stultifying and dangerous of things: normal.

The value of the exercise lies precisely in the extent to which our automatic writing introduces us to feelings that are at odds with those we ordinarily dare to entertain. Much of what we are is dammed up inside us by scruples, a fear of hurting others and embarrassment over what we want when it departs from the expected path. Yet, this neglect of our true selves is also what powers our anxiety, irritability, insomnia and depression – all of these are consequences of not allowing our real thoughts to enter our conscious minds.

Automatic writing will not make us into 'great' writers, but it will do something far more useful: liberate us from some of the insincerities that make us more troubled and restless than we should be. Our chaotic, intense two-minute essays will help us to meet the person we have always been but were too scared to get to know.

49.

How and Why We Catastrophise

The idea of a catastrophiser has an almost comedic ring to it. We picture someone well-meaning but flappable, panicking over something seemingly minor as if the sky were about to cave in. 'There they go again,' we might think, as the catastrophiser insists that 'everything is ruined!' – when in fact the train is just slightly delayed, the keys have been mislaid or they are coming down with a bit of a cold.

But, from close up, there is nothing remotely benign or funny about being the subject of catastrophic thinking. A mind that falls prey to this behaviour can only focus on worst-case scenarios. If an ex-partner is unhappy with them, the direst conclusion is immediate: the ex must be furious with them and bent on revenge and unending torture. As on so many other occasions, the catastrophiser will irresistibly reach for the most awful and pitiless story. In their mind, there is simply no such thing as a 'small' issue.

The catastrophiser may have attained minimal insight into their way of thinking. It seems to be just the way things are. They might find themselves on the receiving end of a great many more or less irate recommendations to simply 'stop worrying'.

What this neglects is that catastrophic thinking tends to have a history. It is almost always a symptom of having encountered a real, full-blown catastrophe somewhere before. It may not be an encounter with a catastrophic *event* so much as familiarity with catastrophic *feelings* – which are generally much easier to lose sight of.

There is a lot of our history bound up in what we catastrophise about, with many individual variations. There are public-opinion catastrophisers who are utterly calm about health matters, and relationship catastrophisers who are totally at ease with money. A couple of questions to ask are: What bit of my past is the catastrophic scenario I fear telling me about? What does the awful thing I dread hint to me about the awful thing I have previously gone through?

Taking the table on the next page as an example, try to recall at least three situations of catastrophising you have experienced, then recreate the table, filling in each of the columns.

Situation	Positive scenario	Suboptimal scenario	Catastrophic scenario	Possible root cause
The letter hasn't arrived yet	The letter is just late	The letter has been lost	The person writing the letter has decided they hate me	Past experiences of being rejected or ignored
I got caught speeding	I'll be let off with a caution	I'll have to pay a fine	I'm definitely going to prison for at least five years	Past experiences of making mistakes and facing severe consequences
I have a big exam coming up	I'll do well in the exam	I'll scrape a pass in the exam	I'm going to fail, lose my place on the course and remain a total failure for the rest of my life	Past experiences of intense scrutiny

We begin to get a handle on our catastrophic imaginations not by being told to be calm or by learning about the theories of the ancient Stoics, but by developing the courage to explore what once went very wrong and learning to more accurately distinguish then from now.

50. How We Hold On to Shame

One of the great problems in the world is also one of the most invisible, because – by its nature – it asks to be hidden and saps our ability to spot its symptoms. But, to generalise grossly, few things so undermine human wellbeing as the sickness of shame.

The guilty feel bad for something specific they have done; the shamed feel wretched simply for being. The affliction lacks borders. As shamed people, we don't connect the myriad ways in which our behaviour and feelings are driven by a base conviction of our own abhorrence. We just take it as a given that we are disgusting. We lack the capacity to imagine that our shame has a history and therefore, perhaps, a future that could be curtailed.

To identify shame triggers, we can reflect on a recent situation in which our response felt disproportionately intense. There are often underlying triggers rooted in past experiences or deeply held beliefs that cause these reactions. A first step in untangling ourselves is to get enough distance to spot and name the problem.

Part 1

1. Consider a recent event in which your reaction seemed out of proportion. What happened? Did you shout, cry or feel the need to leave or shut down?

2. Identify the dominant feelings you experienced immediately after the event. Was there sadness, embarrassment, fury?

3. Were you impulsive or confrontational, or did you want to withdraw or keep quiet?

4. Our intense reactions now can have roots in past traumas. Determine whether the recent event reminds you of a past one. Were your responses similar?

5.   Deeply consider how this event affected your beliefs about yourself. Was there a sense of unworthiness, weakness or being unloved?

6.   Was there a particular situation or person who consistently affected you in this way?

Part 2

Out of ten, rate how true the following statements feel:

I don't deserve to exist.

I am defective.

I am unworthy of being known and loved.

I am a mistake.

I deserve to be abandoned.

I should not be.

Anything rated higher than eight starts to indicate a problem, but if there were an option, most of us in the shamed camp would want to award ourselves 100 or more. This is the windswept, barren land of shame, where many of us have been living all our lives, often without having enough mental wellbeing to know that this is where we have been relegated.

The origins of shame almost always lie in childhood. We suffer from shame because – somewhere in the past – someone else shamed us. What does it take to shame a child? Painfully little. Few people will even realise they are doing it, least of all the victim (unless and until they get a lot of the right help). All you need to do to pulverise a person with shame is to treat their small selves with constant contempt, belittle their efforts to do anything well, berate them powerfully for anything they do wrong, neglect and ignore them, or openly prefer someone else to them.

It takes a very tough and very loving person to be able to get through to the shamed person and tell them in a clear and capable voice what they have always needed to hear: 'You are not a bad person; indeed, you are a very good one. You just had a very bad childhood.'

Illustration List

p. 23
Inkblots similar to those used in the Rorschach psychological test. Spencer Sutton/Science Photo Library.

p. 25
Murrary, Henry A. (1943). 'Thematic Apperception Test'. Harvard University Press (Cambridge, Mass.). Copyright © 1943 by the President and Fellows of Harvard College. Copyright © renewed 1971 by Henry A. Murray. Used by permission. All rights reserved.

p. 25
Edward Hopper, *Chop Suey*, 1929. Oil on canvas, 81.3 × 96.5 cm. Christie's Images/Bridgeman Images. Copyright © Heirs of Josephine Hopper. Licensed by Artists Rights Society (ARS) NY/DACS, London 2026.

p. 28
The Ebbinghaus Optical illusion: The two orange circles are the same size.

p. 36–37
Saul Rosenzweig, illustrations from Picture Frustration Study. From Rosenzweig, S. 1945. The picture-association method and its application in a study of reactions to frustration. *Journal of Personality*, 14, 3–23. Used with permission of John Wiley & Sons. Permission conveyed through Copyright Clearance Center, Inc.

p. 147
Bricklin, B., Piotrowski, Z.A., & Wagner, E.E. (1962). 'The hand test: A new projective test with special reference to the prediction of overt aggressive behaviour'. (Charles C Thomas Publisher, Ltd., Springfield, Illinois).

Text Permissions

p. 17

Excerpt from 'Word Association Text' by Carl Jung, from Long, C.E. (ed.) (1916). *Collected Papers on Analytical Psychology* (Moffat, Yard and Company, New York). © 2007 Foundation of the Works of C.G. Jung, Zürich.

p. 24–26, 34

Murray, H.A. (1937). 'Techniques for a Systematic Investigation of Fantasy', *The Journal of Psychology: Interdisciplinary and Applied*, 3:1, 115–143. (Taylor & Francis, Abingdon).

p. 35

Levis, A.J. (1989). 'The Animal Metaphor Test' from *Conflict Analysis: The Formal Theory of Behaviour: A Theory and Its Experimental Validation* (The Formal Theory Publications Series, v. 1). Normative Publications.

p. 36–37

Rosenzweig, S. 1945. The picture-association method and its application in a study of reactions to frustration. *Journal of Personality*, 14, 3–23. Used with permission of John Wiley & Sons. Permission conveyed through Copyright Clearance Center, Inc.

p. 39–42

Krout, J. (1950). 'Symbol Elaboration Test (S.E.T.): The reliability and validity of a new projective technique' *Psychological Monographs: General and Applied*, 64(4), i–67.

p. 105–107

Drs. John & Julie Gottman, The Four Horsemen & Their Antidotes, The Gottman Institute.

p. 117–118

Reproduced from Oster, G.D., & Gould Crone, P. (2004). Using Drawings in Assessment and Therapy: A Guide for Mental Health. Published by Routledge. © *Oster, G.D., & Gould Crone, P.* 2004. Reproduced by arrangement with Taylor & Francis Group.

p. 146–147

Bricklin, B., Piotrowski, Z.A., & Wagner, E.E. (1962). 'The hand test: A new projective test with special reference to the prediction of overt aggressive behaviour'. (Charles C Thomas Publisher, Ltd., Springfield, Illinois).

p. 169–170

Malchiodi, C. (2007). *The Art Therapy Sourcebook*. 160–161. (McGraw Hill, New York).

p. 173–178

'Testing Your Thoughts'. Adapted from CBT Worksheet Packet © 2024. Beck Institute for Cognitive Behaviour Therapy. Used with permission.

To join The School of Life community and find out more, scan below:

The School of Life publishes a range of books on essential topics in psychological and emotional life, including relationships, parenting, friendship, careers and fulfilment. The aim is always to help us to understand ourselves better and thereby to grow calmer, less confused and more purposeful. Discover our full range of titles, including books for children, here:

www.theschooloflife.com/books

The School of Life also offers a comprehensive therapy service, which complements, and draws upon, our published works:

www.theschooloflife.com/therapy

THESCHOOLOFLIFE.COM